MANAGEMENT
MANTRAS

MANAGEMENT MANTRAS

His Holiness Sri Sri Ravi Shankar

ARKTOS
LONDON 2014

Management Mantras

H. H. Sri Sri Ravi Shankar

1st Edition, February 2013, Sri Sri Publications Trust, Bangalore
1st Reprint, June 2013, Sri Sri Publications Trust, Bangalore
2nd Edition, January 2014, Arktos Media Ltd., London

Printed in the United Kingdom.

ISBN 978-1-907166-22-8

BIC classification:
Management: leadership and motivation (KJMB)
Hinduism (HRG)

ARKTOS MEDIA LTD
www.arktos.com

Contents

Chapter 1

Introduction

I know the mantra for meditation.
What is a management mantra?

Management begins in the mind. When the mind manages itself better, it can manage anything.

Human life is a combination of the concrete and the abstract. Our body is concrete and our mind is abstract. Both positive and negative thoughts emanate from the same brain. We know very little about ourselves. Being better aware of our own mind helps us to understand life better.

Human life is structured just like an atom. At the centre of the atom is the proton and a field of negative charges orbits it. Similarly, we too have virtues at the centre of our being. But if we have not realised these virtues, we roam the outer orbits. So we need to take it for granted that we already have these virtues within us.

Always remember you are a citizen of the world, the whole

world belongs to you. There is some virtue to be learnt from every part of the world — teamwork from Japan, precision from Germany, marketing and negotiation skills from the United States, courtesy, decency and refinement from the British, and human values from the villages of India. You will find good qualities everywhere in the world. You too possess these qualities. They only need nourishment.

If you are committed to doing something to uplift life around you, if you are committed to compassion, to creativity, then the world will be a wonderful place. More often than not, we are stuck in our own mindsets. If we could put ourselves in others' shoes, we would be able to see their point of view. We need to keep changing and attempting different roles.

In any organisation, top management should be setting goals to define what is to be achieved. Middle management should deal with how and when the goals need to be fulfilled. Lower management should concern itself with the execution of the means to achieve the goals and ensure the quality of the output. People at the top of the hierarchy need to be expansion-conscious while those at the bottom need to be quality-conscious. But all these levels should work together in harmony. This is the sign of a healthy institution.

An important part of management is creativity. All CEOs and Chairmen want to improve their enterprise, but they sideline research and development — the most creative part of the enterprise. They assume that this is to be done outside the orbit of their enterprise.

Creativity can only come from silence. If we maintain two minutes of silence every day, then we will see that a whole new dimension of life opens up.

Chapter 2

Key Points of
Effective Management

*Do we really understand the difference
between motivation and inspiration?*

By and large, employees in various enterprises are motivated
to perform better by the annual increment. Sometimes, an
additional incentive is given during certain festivals. This is
especially true in developing countries. But such approaches are
short-lived and have a temporary effect because the motivation
comes from outside.

Inspiration on the other hand, which comes from within, is
more effective and long-lasting. When people are inspired in the
workplace, they work enthusiastically and do an excellent job.

We have conducted workshops in many organisations around
the world, such as the World Bank and Shell Oil and many more.
We call this workshop APEX — Achieving Personal Excellence.
It has had amazing results! People who have attended it have

developed abundant energy and great enthusiasm. They have re-discovered their inspiration to work with a sense of belongingness, because now they have been taught how to handle stress.

Bangalore in India is called the IT city. I have a different expansion for IT. It is Inner Transformation.

Inner motivation and inner transformation comes to people who are inspired to achieve excellence.

So how does one tap into the energy required to achieve such inner transformation?

There are four sources of energy — food, sleep, breath and a calm mind.

If you don't believe food is a source of energy, you should fast for one or two days and see what happens. The second source of energy is sleep. If we don't sleep well, we can't work well. The third is our breath, which we have not paid any attention to, because nobody taught us about the importance of breath. And the fourth is a meditative mind, a calm and serene mental state.

Chapter 3

Attributes of a Good Leader

A true leader lets go of control...
he creates leaders, not followers.

An important mark of good leadership is letting go of control. Are you in control when you are sleeping or when you are dreaming? Can you control any other function in your body? Your heart pumps oxygen on its own. Are you in control of your thoughts? You are not.

So, when you realise you really do not have any hold over all the critical aspects of your life, then you learn that the idea that you are in control is an illusion. And knowing this will relax you.

Sets Examples
A leader leads by example. He does not just issue orders. He teaches others how to do things by first doing them himself. A good leader creates leaders, not followers. He takes good care of those whom

he is leading. He delegates responsibility.

Does not Worry About Position

A good leader is well aware that the respect that he gains through virtue is very different from the respect he gains through the position he enjoys. He knows that the respect the position brings is short-lived and temporary. Being a chairman of a committee or a president of another, being a governor or a barrister — these are all momentary experiences. Positions come and go.

But the respect that he gets for being a nice person, for his virtues and attitude, is genuine. It lasts long.

Accepts Challenges

A good leader is motivated when there are challenges to meet. He is alert in times of crisis. He is not disturbed, rather he sees challenges as opportunities.

Balances Head and Heart

A successful leader maintains a balance by listening to the head as well as the heart. When he needs to commit himself to his work, he listens to his head. In other areas of his life, he listens to his heart.

Is Empathetic

An effective leader is able to put himself in others' shoes and see things from their point of view. He is a good communicator.

Does not Care for Comfort

Anything creative and dynamic can happen only when you stretch yourself beyond your comfort zone. You are often stuck here. You may think that you cannot do something. But if you make an effort and take that first step ahead, then you will find that you are not bound by your comfort zone. A good leader knows this.

Has Long-term Vision

A true leader has a long term vision and the short term plans to work on it. He is prepared to put the organisation, the country, before his own needs. That sense of sacrifice is needed.

Has Integrity

A good leader is *satyadarshi* (truthful), *samdarshi* (equanimous), *priyadarshi* (pleasant personality), *pardarshi* (transparent) and *doordarshi* (farsighted). He has a mission and a vision and a spirit of sacrifice, compassion and commitment.

Does not let His Position Make Him Arrogant

A good leader does not exhibit that he is a leader. He becomes one among everybody. He does not think he is better than everybody else. He just sees himself as part of the group. A sense of belongingness makes him interact with the ones he leads. Developing good human relationship skills is a necessary quality in a successful leader.

My teacher — Pandit Sudhakar Chaturvedi — was a close associate of Mahatma Gandhi. He travelled with him, writing letters for him as well as teaching him the Bhagavad Gita.

Once, Mahatma Gandhi was travelling with a group of people in a train in the hilly regions of Darjeeling in India. Darjeeling is a hill station and the train was moving uphill. Suddenly, the engine came detached from the coaches. The engine continued ahead but all the coaches started rolling backwards down the gradient!

It took a little while for people to realise what was happening. The engine-less train was gaining momentum because of the gradient. So there was chaos. Everybody was screaming and praying! They could not even jump out of the moving train because they would fall thousands of metres down. Everyone was in panic mode.

During this time, Mahatma Gandhi was dictating letters for my teacher to take down. Gandhiji did not know the south

Indian languages but my teacher did, so he would take dictation and translate. My teacher asked him whether he was aware of the situation, told him that there was no guarantee that they would be alive in a short while. The train could fall at any moment because there was no engine attached and it was out of control.

Gandhiji replied that if they were saved, they would have wasted so much time in anxiety. Whatever was to happen could not be controlled; hence it was better that they wrote their letters. That was the lesson that he gave my teacher.

Even in moments of utter danger, a person like Mahatma Gandhi remained totally involved in his work.

Today, those who are very aggressive are the leaders in schools and colleges. Aggression is linked to pride. This is unfortunate. Compassion, equanimity, caring and love need to be attached to pride. This was how it was in the earlier days. Then, if somebody lost his or her temper it would be considered wrong. This was because a calm and pleasant state of mind was considered to be an essential quality in a leader.

Someone who could take on the stress of others and give them a reason to smile was seen as a true leader. We have heard many stories about Lord Buddha's unshakeable smile or composure. Mahatma Gandhi showed the same trait. He had a very firm and steady mind, nobody could disturb his equanimity.

We see such managers in companies. They don't give in to emotion, they have a calm mind. They can take on challenges and handle them better. Those who are not impulsive show better, clearer perception. This is what is expected of a leader — better perception, clear observation and graceful expression.

Psychologists today say that our attention span is decreasing because we watch too much television. This bombards the mind with too many impressions so that it is unable to focus for long. Children show an attention-deficit syndrome. They have not been taught how to relax their minds. When the mind is relaxed, the attention span increases. If you observe yourself on a Sunday morning, you will note that you are very sharp. But on a Wednesday or a Thursday, when you have just come home from work in the evening, or when you are very tired, your attention span is poorer.

A leader is one who has the patience to listen to those working under him. He is capable of seeing others' points of view as well. I would call this a multi-dimensional understanding of a situation or a person. Seeing an event from various angles gives you the complete picture.

Chapter 4

Methods of Developing Leadership Skills

*A leader thinks of himself as a
perpetual student, and he learns from everybody,
even a child.*

Celebration, relaxation, a sense of belonging, and the need to regularly upgrade our skills and acquire new ones — these are priorities that we should never neglect. Everyone is a student throughout their life. This is another quality of leadership. A leader never stops learning. He thinks of himself as a perpetual student, and he learns from everybody, even from a child.

Creating Trust
If you look at the people around you and tell them that you do not trust them, then how will you feel? How would you like to live in a world where you do not trust anybody and nobody trusts you? You would feel lonely, sad, insecure, helpless, miserable, depressed, or angry, all the time. Just imagine living in a world where everyone is

like that. Would you be able to make any progress?

First, you need to create trust. That is the secret of management! And if you cannot trust others, the same thing applies to you. Nobody likes being doubted. So why do we keep doubting everyone around us?

Let me give you an everyday example. In Europe or America, you find a caution notice, a label, pasted inside cars, basically cautioning you to drive carefully, warning you that rash driving can be fatal. If you look around carefully, you realise that you are cautioned about every other thing in the world. This has made us lose our innate trust in goodness. You will notice that our doubts are always about something that is positive. If somebody tells you, "I love you very much," you ask, "Really?" But if somebody says, "I hate you", you do not question it! Because hate, you think, is natural.

So the next time you doubt, examine your thought. In all probability, it must be something good that you are skeptical about. That is why we doubt God. We doubt in the goodness of people, in compassion, in love, in anything that is sweet. When we taught our courses free of cost, people would doubt. "They must be getting something. Why are they teaching for free?" It sounds too good to be true!

This sort of paranoia has been prevalent in society for long. And it is only spirituality that can take us away from these false alarms and fears, and take us towards trusting ourselves and the people around us.

There is goodness to be found in every field. Not all corporate bigwigs are corrupted. Not all politicians are hopeless and not all spiritual and religious leaders are bad. All that we need is to be able to see the goodness within ourselves and to trust that the Divine will bring all that we need into our lives.

Banks give credit. I just take credit. I go to the bank knowing that they always give credit. Take a burning lamp for instance. It is not just the lamp that burns. The wick and the oil burn too, but the lamp takes the credit. Any achievement is a collective effort of so many. Spirituality is the connecting link, the one inspiration, the one wave, the one energy, the one divinity that helps us progress — that component of life is called the spiritual component.

And it is the lack of a spiritual component that throws us either into violence on one side or into depression and suicidal tendencies on the other side.

Developing a Sense of Belonging

You need to see your life in context of time and space — how vast creation is, how big the universe is and how small your life is, relative to the cosmos. Billions of years have passed and billions more are to come. You are one among six billion people on this planet right now. Do you feel you belong to them all? Do you feel at home with everyone? You can. Then, the moment you have a sense of belonging (starting with the feeling), just know that you have won customers everywhere. In fact, they become your family, an extended family. A sense of belonging is very necessary in any set-up, whether it is a corporation, an NGO, a social or religious organisation. A good leader must create this sense of belonging, a sense of responsibility.

Communicating Through Presence

We convey more through our presence than through our words. A baby looking at you does not have to say, 'I love you'. The baby does not have to verbalise things. As adults, we talk and talk away, arguing for an hour, and yet we see that the person with whom we are arguing is not convinced. Or even if we feel we have convinced them, they are in the same place as before! All our logic and our convictions, all our power has failed and we feel frustrated in life. But this happens because we have not used the dimension that lies within us, i.e. non-verbal communication.

You should know this — you convey so much through your presence, your feelings. When you get out of an aeroplane, the air hostesses tell you to have a nice day. They do not mean it personally, but when the same words come to you from your mother or grandmother, something touches you deeply. You feel their words carry some emotion, some feelings. So your words must carry them too. If your presence is all mumbo jumbo, jammed with anger, pent-up and negative emotions, you cannot communicate properly, effectively and freely with people.

The key to success for anyone in this world is effective communication conveying the intended meaning, timely two-way communication. Do not just say whatever you feel is right and walk away. Make sure that the person has received and digested your message and responded to it. It is your ability to evoke a reciprocal response from whoever you are communicating with, and this will not happen unless you are truly integrated in your own life.

So I would say that it is every individual's birthright to have a disease-free body, a quiver-free breath, a confusion-free mind, an inhibition-free intellect, a trauma-free memory and an ego which is not constrained but which encompasses everyone. And I would give the term 'spirituality' to anything that provides all these. I see it as a force which does not allow anything or anyone to take the smile away from you. We need to be able to smile through any adverse situation!

Having Freedom at the Workplace

When you are at peace with yourself, you can re-create this peace in your workspace and the work culture will also improve. You will need to give some thought to how you can create an easy and informal atmosphere for others around you at work. When you walk in and out of the office, you always get a greeting. Are these genuine or superficial? Most of the pleasantries we exchange come from a superficial level; greetings like 'Thank you very much', or

'You did a good job' or 'Have a nice day.'

The entire work environment is filled with such superficial, sometimes even hypocritical greetings. How can you expect such an environment to produce the results you are looking for? When the President of the World Bank met me, he asked what the secret of my success was and how I got so much work done with so little money at my disposal. I told him that it was not just the money that did it but something more. It was the freedom at the workplace.

In the span of just one year, 3,000 volunteers adopted 21,000 villages in India, in the 5H programme. This was done incurring an expenditure of only two crore rupees. Nobody could believe it but it did happen. They could construct roads, provide proper drinking water and do many more things with that amount. And it is purely due to the dedication and inspiration of those involved.

We should know the difference between motivation and inspiration. We can motivate somebody by giving them a few hundred rupees, but such motivation is short-lived. It will only last two or three months. After that, they will want some money again. If people are not inspired from within, it will not be possible to build a good work ethic. Work culture revolves around either inspiration or emergency deadlines or fear psychosis. And if such fear psychosis is created in people, it works for some time, but it is not a healthy thing in the long run. Today, many of our work set-ups increasingly run on fear psychosis. To meet deadlines, it is this insecurity that we need to lose, rather than the motivation.

Developing the Right Mindset

Our mindset is the next thing we need to attend to. I think there are two kinds — one is the labour union mind and the other is the authoritarian mind.

The labour union mind tends to point a finger at others. Such a person may feel that the manager is not good enough, that the senior is not nice — he does not let the juniors take their own decisions. If your mind is in the present moment, it will stop complaining. Your complaining is a product of your unconscious mind.

The authoritarian-minded person always feels that only he can do something, that no one else is as efficient or capable as he is. In this country, right from ancient times, we have been very good at delegating. Though there is one God, we have divided God into creator, manager and transformer — Brahma, Vishnu, and Mahesh. We have allocated three important portfolios to women — finance to Lakshmi, education to Saraswati and defence to Durga.

Delegation is important but it can only happen when you step out of the authoritarian mindset. Such a mindset does not allow the leader to take responsibility for making others work. This is on the managerial level. So if he does not trust anybody with work, how will he motivate or inspire the team to sustain their efforts?

Realising Dreams
It is very important to dream. But there has to be a fine balance between practicality and dreams. When you are given certain tasks, you find that they get done because of your *atmik shakti*, along with your *sankalpa shakti*. *Sankalpa* is your determination.

Once I had announced that I would go to Pakistan. But I had no visa till the last day. Our people talked to many people but everyone was discouraging. They urged me not to go. The Pakistani authorities had found out that I had an Israeli stamp in my passport. Islamabad follows a policy of not granting a visa if the applicant's passport has an Israeli stamp in it. So people began to wonder what was going to happen because a big programme had already been arranged for me in Islamabad and Karachi.

But it happened! I insisted that I just had to go. And I got the visa because I was bent on it. I got it at 4 p.m. and took the 6 p.m. flight. The Pakistani High Commissioner and I were in the same place, where the SAARC meeting was going on in Pakistan, and even he was amazed as to how I had obtained the visa!

The human mind assumes that it works in isolation, but the truth is that there is some other force also at work. You can move ahead and achieve all you want against all odds. You just have to have the faith.

There was another incident. One evening, a big *satsang* had been planned in Ambala. But it had been raining all day. The organisers had the faith that if we had planned an evening *satsang*, the rain would stop by then. And their conviction was such that there was no rain in the evening and we had a great *satsang*. And this has happened not once but over and over again! Nature supports you when you have the conviction.

It was Guru Gobind Singh Ji who revived this culture in our country. The entire country is indebted to him. He told us to work like warriors. It is this warrior-like quality which is needed if we wish to realise our dreams. Unfortunately, our corporate culture is clogged by a comfort zone attitude. We prefer to live in our own comfort zone and not be adventurous. We do not want to stretch ourselves a little more than we think we can. We need to inspire people around us, to push them a little to make them do what they can do.

I want to give you another example. I was told that there is a certain place, a village in China, where they make only buttons. The buttons on our shirts are all made in China. This one village monopolises the production of buttons. We may feel that manufacturing of buttons is a small industry. But it is a wonder the way the industry has grown and that village has become strong. This kind of phenomenon was common in India too but it is not seen much anymore. Different communities specialising in different things is a practise that can boost our economy, our self confidence; it can benefit the morale of our people.

Having Trust in Human Values

The basis of science is trust in mathematics. If there is no trust in mathematics, then science cannot move forward at all. Likewise, business cannot progress if the industry shows no trust in customers and customers in their creditors. Human values are about trusting the good nature we all are inherently endowed with.

Half our health is spent in gaining wealth and then half that wealth is spent in gaining back the health we have lost in the process! I don't think that is good economics. We do not need to cultivate human values. It is our very nature. What really obstructs human values is stress and tension. If a person is under strain, then his perception, observation and expression suffer.

And there are only two ways to get rid of strain — either the work load needs to be lessened or energy levels need to improve. In today's world, it is not possible to lessen the amount of work. It will always only increase.

So, the solution is to increase your energy. There are four different sources of energy.

The first is food, of the right quality and quantity.

The second is sleep, adequate and sound.

The third is a meditative state of mind.

The fourth is the most important. It is the breath — something that we have ignored or forgotten. 90 percent of impurities in the system are thrown out of the body through the breath. Every time we exhale, we get rid of carbon dioxide. Toxins are being ejected from the system and our blood is being purified. The breath is such a vital source of energy and yet we have not done much to learn about it.

The breath is the link between the body and the mind. For every emotion, there is a corresponding rhythm in the breath. The breathing pattern is different for one who is depressed, unhappy, anxious and tense.

I have taken this notion to different environments, including prisons. About 60,000 prisoners around the world have practised the breathing exercises we taught, over five days, for a couple of hours each day. They have experienced an amazing effect and then wondered why they did not do these exercises earlier. They felt that their lives would have been different and that perhaps they would not have been in prison at all!

When emotions take control, on the spur of the moment a person may commit a crime. By the time he comes to his senses, he would have already done wrong and may not even know why he did it!

The mind oscillates between the past and the future — between being angry about the past or being anxious about the future. This continuously generates many toxins in the body. Healthy breathing is the key to eliminating these toxins and harmonising emotions. Neither at home nor in school have we heard or learned anything about managing our emotions. The ancient Vedic or yogic systems (Yoga and the Korean Tai Chi) used breathing techniques for this. They formulated breathing and other exercises which release tension and improve alertness and awareness. I feel it is very important to teach our children and our people how they should handle their negative feelings and emotions such as anger, jealousy and hatred.

The business industry today is badly affected by hatred — religious hatred which resulted in the 9/11 catastrophe and all the subsequent wars. I feel the root cause of all this is a lack of understanding and tolerance. And this is the result of growing up in a particular religious tradition and being convinced that it is the only way to salvation.

There is no multi-religious and multi-cultural education. We accept food from every part of the world. We eat Chinese food. We do not have to be Danish to eat Danish cookies nor do we become Swiss if we eat Swiss chocolates. We also accept music from every part of the world. So too, do we accept technology. Then, why don't we accept wisdom from every part of the world and from every tradition?

I feel all those unfortunate people in Afghanistan must not have had an opportunity to learn about other traditions and cultures. If, as children, we were given a little education about all the different religious and spiritual traditions, such as Hinduism, Buddhism, Christianity etc. then we would grow up to be more broad-minded in our thinking. We would feel a sense of belonging with everybody around us.

Nurturing a Scientific Temperament

Science is about learning 'what something is' and spirituality is about knowing 'who I am'. The two never contradicted each other, at least not in the East. 5,000 years ago, a rishi had said that by thoroughly studying one atom, you can become free. If you truly understand any one substance, you become free. If you can know what is contained in one little particle of this universe, then that is what the whole universe is all about. That is what got me interested me in physics. He also spoke about ancient Vedic times and how they connect with today's quantum mechanics, theory of relativity, principles of karma etc.

We need a scientific temperament, whether it is in trade, tradition, truth or technology. All these arenas need to be upgraded and reviewed from time to time. And I think we need to infuse human values in every such area in the world today. It has become urgent. Even if a small part of the world is allowed to remain ignorant and without a complete outlook on life, humanity and wisdom, the world will not be the same.

Effective Communication Skills

It is an art to express our opinion in a way that will be appreciated. Those who possess this ability to communicate effectively and impressively are unique. To communicate affectionately and without prejudice with one and all is a skill worth possessing.

When you come across a person who knows more than you do, you should listen attentively to him. When you come across someone who seems less knowledgeable than you, you should be humble and strive to make him as informed as or even better informed than you. When you talk with elderly people, you must bear in mind that one day you too will become old. On the other hand, talk with a person of your age group as if you were his best friend.

Most of us are not good listeners really. When we listen to somebody, the speaker's very first sentence triggers some conversation within us. A good listener is always a good speaker and later on, he will definitely become a good leader.

This world is varied beyond our imagination. There is always something to share, learn and teach. We need to attract as many people as we can, with our ability to communicate with them.

Building a Team

These five principles will help you build a strong and effective team:

- Never underestimate your team members. If you do, you will not be able to win their trust.

- Defend your intentions and not your actions. Often people defend their actions and lose sight of their intentions. Then they feel sorry and weak. There is no need to feel sorry. You should defend your intention to do right.

- With teamwork you will achieve more than you can individually. Some kinds of work are best done alone, and some others, as part of a team. You should find a balance between working alone and working in a team. In either case, you will face obstacles. The skill lies in not developing an aversion to either and instead, focusing on the goal.

- Do not defend someone's mistakes. It does not do justice to the team and stops the person from learning. Soft-heartedness and misplaced compassion in an organisation can be detrimental to teamwork and productivity in the organisation.

- Never justify a mistake using intimidation or logic. Raising your voice and asserting through intimidation may make a wrong appear right, but will not fool anyone for long.

Experiencing Freedom in all Roles

Many people do not want to work under someone else, be it in their personal sphere, as an employee in a company or even as a volunteer. They have the notion that when they work under someone, they lose their freedom and have to be accountable.

Thus, many people opt to run a business of their own, wanting to be their own boss. But even if you have your own business, you are answerable to so many people. If you cannot be accountable to even one person, how can you be accountable to many? This is the paradox. In fact, having your own business binds you more than having a boss does!

Refusing to work under someone is a sign of weakness and not strength. A strong person will feel comfortable working under anyone. This is because he knows his strength. It is the weak and poor in spirit who do not like to work under someone else because they are unaware of their own strength. They cannot be successful in business or in any profession.

One who is timid and weak in spirit would feel uncomfortable working even for a wise person, but one who knows his own strength can work effectively even for a fool! Such a person can turn every disadvantage into an advantage using his skill and intelligence. Even a fool can bring out the best in your communication skills!

Many of us crave freedom from the circumstances, situations

or people surrounding us, but that is not freedom at all. Knowing that nobody can take away your freedom is your strength. And realising that will help you work better, under someone or on your own, and will also help you enjoy your work.

Bringing in Steadiness in Dynamism
Often, you are in a hurry in life. At such times, you are unable to perceive things properly. Your haste blinds you to the thrill and beauty of life. You can never be close to the truth when you are in a rush because your perception, observation and expression become distorted.

This kind of constant haste robs life of its joy and denies you the happiness and freedom of the present moment. Often, you do not even know why you are in a hurry. It almost becomes a biological phenomenon to be in a rush. You should wake up and become aware of the rush in you!

It is also ridiculous to be in a rush to slow down. You just need to become aware of the rush and it will take care of itself. Slowing down does not mean procrastinating or being lethargic, though it is easy to get caught up in the extremes of either speeding through things or being lethargic. Rushing is caused by feverishness, and feverishness arises out of deficiency — a need to achieve. Dynamism though, is a natural expression of fulfilment.

The golden rule is to be awake. When you are awake, you cannot help but be dynamic.

Chapter 5

Innovation

*Innovation has to become a part of
our everyday life — whether
at the workplace or in our homes.*

I was told the theme of this conference is 'Innovation, Entrepreneurship and Social Business'. Just yesterday I was at the Economic Times Awards and I happened to listen to two professors from Harvard. They listed about eight points in the presentation, explaining how a brewery in South Africa has excelled, then how other companies around the world have excelled. And after that, they listed another seven items, and I turned around to Prof. R. K. Pachauri who was sitting next to me, and I said to him, "We already do these things." What were those things? They said, "Bring in team work, bring out a commitment in people, a work and life balance — moderating the amount of stress in their lives so that they do not burn out, encourage the concept of participation among people." Many among the audience there, the successful businessmen, I tell you, some of them have not even completed their educational degree, but they have done very well in India. So, what is the secret behind their success story? How did they make it? All that the Harvard professors were saying, these achievers sitting in the audience had already implemented in their businesses. It is interesting to know.

The first step to success is innovation. See, when innovation is a natural quality, a personality trait in you, it comes up in every aspect of your life. Innovation should be a part of your behaviour too, not just your profession. We have a rural development programme and within that programme, we have volunteers who come up with some really innovative concepts — sometimes even in as simple a task as making small carry bags. They will come up with something creative, going beyond the common prototype.

Once when I was in America, when we had about 500 volunteers who had assembled for a *satsang*, I told them, "Look, creativity is a part of Divinity. Now you have to invoke that Divinity inside you. You have two months' time. You have to do something creative." And everyone came up with a different project, and each one was very creative. One person came up with 'ice-cream made without eggs', another with 'ice-cream without chemicals', and there were a host of other innovative consumer products on display. Then there was one lady — she was 60 years old — she did a project on making handkerchiefs. She enumerated 17 points to her credit saying how her handkerchief was the best in the world. It was mindboggling. And everybody was laughing and exclaiming about how someone could be so creative in things like making a handkerchief, I mean who would have thought of that? So you see, innovation has to ooze from our behaviour. When you go home from work in the evening, if you like making a sandwich, do not make the same sandwich every day. Declare the next week a week of innovation, do something new. I sometimes go into the kitchen to cook but I never cook the same meal. It is always an experiment. Of course, there is a risk. Innovation goes hand in hand with risk. Sometimes it can turn out well, at other times, things may not go so successfully. Most of the times, it turns out wonderful. If you use your intuition, your innovation will succeed almost every time. And it brings you immense satisfaction. So, innovation has to become a part of our everyday life, whether it is to do with music, or any form of art, or cooking, or even in the way you conduct the meeting at your workplace. It does not always have to be the same thing.

Once I was a chief guest at a library meeting in Jaipur. I thought the organiser was quite tired. The general secretary of that organising committee was going in and out of the room. He never heard the talk. When it came to offering a vote of thanks, he wanted to come and garland me. I jumped right in and took the garland from him and said, "Look, he worked so hard and he has sacrificed even listening or sitting and meditating. He needs all the congratulations and attention of people because he has sacrificed his participation at the cost of completing all the arrangements." He was shocked. My point is, you need to bring in certain changes, create some dynamism in your everyday life and that is a true sign of being a lively human being. We are not machines, we do not have to work in a mechanical manner. We need to be innovative. And the innovation should be very personal, very unique to each individual. As I said earlier, there are two aspects to innovation — taking a risk and then playing safe. You borrow a sum of 10 lakhs from your father and say, "I am going to be innovative," and then you just spend all that money and come up with nothing. That is not ok. So you have to play safe. Entrepreneurship must, necessarily, combine risk and safety.

I will now tell you about The Art of Living. The Art of Living is a volunteer-based organisation. And when it is volunteer-based, there is no interference. Everybody does the kind of work that they want to do, what they think is correct. And to manage a group of volunteers is the most difficult thing. Our apex bodies and organisers have great experience doing just that. They cannot hire anybody because everybody is their own boss. The skill lies in coordinating this whole group in which everyone thinks that they know best about what is needed. It is a challenge to work in this environment. It can cause a lot of frustration. And especially in a spiritual organisation, where you cannot be frustrated! If you are frustrated, you are told, "You have to go and meditate, do not work now." You will be given many knowledge lectures. So you cannot be angry, you cannot be frustrated, you cannot get upset because after all, you are teaching the world how not to get stressed, how not to get upset, how to accommodate and how to be human, how to exhibit all the human values. Don't you agree that this is a big challenge?

Once in a while, we do call a meeting of organisers. There, you should watch the fun. Everyone comes up with their own great ideas. Now you know what they say about a spiritual organisation, that charity cannot happen out of an empty bowl. So when we do a lot of charitable projects, we have to raise funds too. So, one gentleman came up with the great idea of making *bidis* (cheap, locally made cigarettes). Just imagine a spiritual organisation producing *bidis* because it offers employment to so many womenfolk in a village. They roll the tobacco *bidis* and then sell them in the manufacturer's own name. If there is Ganesha *bidi,* why should there not be Swamiji *bidi*. You can imagine that this "innovative, very promising business which can help up to ten schools in one go" had to be stopped right there! Because it does not go with the ethics of any spiritual organisation to encourage, even remotely, anything of that nature. But volunteers of course come up with these great ideas in the name of innovation.

So, this is how the organiser of an NGO, of a volunteer-based organisation, becomes really skillful. I think after you complete your MBA course, at least for 3-4 months, even 6 months, you must work in one of any number of NGOs in the world. You can learn many practical skills and also learn to manage people in a diverse age group (right from youth to elderly people), learn to manage varied mental tendencies, educational backgrounds, professional backgrounds, basically people coming together from all walks of life. Running an NGO is a tall task. And it is truly very interesting. It brings out the best in you. When you face challenges, you become more innovative. Creativity will not come to you out of the blue, while you may be sitting in Harvard or some similar place, if you are not interacting with people. Your interaction with the public, with groups of people, is absolutely essential.

Recently, the United Nations Millennium Campaign asked the Art of Living to be their partner, so we said, "Ok, we will do it." Just two months ago the Stand Up and Speak Out event took place in all the countries where there is not much UN presence. Our volunteers could really bring up the issue to its fullest there, in countries like Surinam, Trinidad, Madagascar, and many other places. Of 37 million people who stood up, 7 million were volunteers from The Art of Living alone, who spoke without much effort. What can bring people to participate in social business is an inspiration, a genuineness. When a genuine spirit of caring and sharing surges in you, you will find a field created especially for you, a social field. There is a joy in getting but there is the greatest joy in giving, in contributing. The mother at home enjoys serving people. She cooks many dishes and serves them happily, when her children come home. If she is all by herself, she does not prepare 10 types of dishes and eat them all by herself. Though she is an expert cook, her joy comes from feeding others. This is a mature kind of joy. We were all born with an instinct of grabbing, of experiencing joy, but we should not die with the same basic instinct alone. We must mature, for there is nothing like sharing joy that brings satisfaction, nothing else can give you that much fulfillment. The need to be happy oneself, but equally to make everyone around us happy too, is a concept that we must constantly factor into our lives.

In the Gita, there is a saying:

> *Prasaade sarva duhkhaanaam haanirasyopajaayate*
> *Prasanna chetaso hyaashu buddhih paryavatishthate*
> *Naasti buddhir ayuktasya na chaayuktasya bhaavanaa;*
> *Na chaa bhaavayatah shaantir ashaantasya kutah sukham.*

When your mind is at peace, your intellect becomes sharp. If your mind is clogged with a million worries or desires or sorrows, you are unable to achieve anything. Some calmness in the mind, some pleasantness, is essential for the mind to function at its best. Do you know why children are so sharp? It is because they are happy. As you grow up and as your happiness graph declines, that is when your ability to learn and imbibe also declines. You smile less. It is spirituality that makes you smile, that allows you to keep the smile that nobody can take away from you, and not just when you greet somebody, but a genuine, lasting smile that springs from the depth of your mind, your heart. That is *prasanna chetaso* — a pleasant mind.

Prasanna chetaso hyaashu buddhih paryavatishthate — The intellect becomes sharper, then it gets re-established.

Naasti buddhir ayuktasya na chaayuktasya bhaavanaa — If you are not coordinated within yourself, if you are not integrated within, if body, mind, breath, awareness, life, is haphazard, then neither is there any intellectual growth, nor is there harnessed emotion. And in the absence of both these, there cannot be peace. When there is no peace, there is no happiness. This is what Lord Krishna says to Arjuna. Right in the battlefield. Life itself is a battlefield. Every day there is something or the other that we need to battle with. And how you can be centred is all that you need to worry about. The rest — innovation, entrepreneurship and everything else — will spring from it.

Take a pause to see what is happening in your mind, right

at this moment. See whether your attention is directed at me or at what I am saying. Now, focus on yourself for a bit. So far I was the scenery, you were the seer. Now turn your attention from the scenery to the seer. When you turn away from everything on the outside, instead focusing on your self, that is what centredness is. This is the first sutra of yoga, *Yoga Chitta Vritti Nirodhaha*. What happens then? *Tada drishtu swarupeva sthaanam* — getting back to the seer is what happens when the mind settles down. Yoga is not just exercise, it is getting away from the object to the subject. And it happens just like that, in a minute. Taking your mind inward, that is extremely energising. And that is meditation. Even if we close our eyes, we do not shut our mind. Our mind is constantly flying all over the place, thinking about what all we did or all that we still want to do. Meditation is this distilled moment, taking attention from what I have done or what I want to do to what I am. This exercise will enhance our intelligence, our capabilities.

We were once in a school in Dharavi, I had just inaugurated the opening of the school. Seeing the poor kids from the Dharavi slum, I thought, many of them will become so brilliant that they will go to IIT to study. In our country, we have this technology; we have these resources to enhance our memory, our innovation, our intelligence. Our country can lead the world in these aspects. It is so unfortunate that we do not value what we have. Especially those who have studied more than others around them have, they think they know a lot. Real education is to make you aware that the more you know, the more you will be baffled, the more you will say, "I do not know, I know very little". Innovation has taught us a lot. Yet we know very little about our universe. What we see is only a tiny part, a rather insignificant part of what we do not know.

Uncertainty in Business

You must have, at some point, seen how people fish in water. (As businessmen, you do know how to fish in troubled waters!)

So when you go fishing, what do you notice? The moment you take that body (fish) out of the water, there is no life left in it. That fish struggles for a few seconds and then collapses. The eyes are still there, looking at you with a blank stare, but with no life in them. When under water, this very fish was moving, expressing life. So now tell me, where is the life of the fish to be found? Is it in the body or in the water? That's a question for you. If its life is in the water, then that means its body is only exhibiting signs of that life. The same is true for all our human bodies. If your human body is taken out of this atmosphere, 200 miles above this planet earth, it will shrink like the fish. Your eyes too would still be there, staring, but there would be no life in them. So now where is your life contained? Is it in this shell-like body or is it in the air that is all around you? You simply have to sit and reflect on this. You will realise that your life is not really within this body, rather it is all over, all around you.

This also explains the phenomenon of phantom limbs. How many of you know that there is a medical phenomenon called phantom limbs? When a person gets his arm or leg amputated, he does not have that limb afterwards, but he still feels pain and itching in the place where his arm or leg once was. Have you heard about this? Even after the limb is lost, there is this sensation of pain in that part where there is no leg at all anymore. Doctors are unable to explain why this happens. It's in the mind, in the brain. When such a person does meditation, he realises that he is made up of not just his body, but also the spirit, and upon this realisation, the phantom limb problem disappears. This has been witnessed in thousands of cases.

Our body is like the wick of a candle and our mind is like the glowing light all around the wick. Just as a candle lives on oxygen, the flame needs oxygen to keep burning — if you cover the candle with a glass, the light remains only as long as oxygen is present. The moment the oxygen runs out, the flame is extinguished. In the same way, we are also completely dependent on oxygen, or what we may call the life force. This life force is what our ancestors called the *atma*, the *jivatma*.

Are you still reading the words on this page? You know, when someone talks in deeply scientific or philosophical language, the mind just takes a break and goes for a cappuccino! But if you are a thorough scientist, you truly understand spirituality. If you know about dark matter, dark energy, if you know about the origin of universe, if you reflect on the magnanimity of this universe, you will become spiritual. In our universe, there are millions of black holes floating around, escaping the Sun. You cannot insure against these black holes. A black hole can swallow the entire galaxy at any point of time. We live in a most dangerous universe, a most uncertain universe. The size of a black hole may be the same as that of a peanut, but at any time, it can swallow whole, the entire solar system. And the entire universe, in a moment, could go into complete annihilation. Many of us live our lives, unaware of this.

But being aware of this phenomenon, the uncertainty of life gives you enormous strength. Usually people believe that uncertainty makes you shaky. But let me tell you, when you know that there is nothing certain in this magnificent universe — that any meteoroid can come hurtling down at any time and hit planet Earth, that one day, we would all be gone then like the dinosaurs, if you think about this, you will be able to smile easily. For it would be an end to all the problems, all the uncertainties we face in our lives surely! It is said that planet Jupiter absorbs all the meteoroids; it is saving planet Earth from all such objects coming in the direction of the earth. Our sages have said this a long time ago — that it is planet Jupiter, or *Guru Grah*, which is saving planet Earth.

What I mean to say is, as young businessmen, what really shakes you most is the uncertainty, isn't it? Isn't that your biggest worry? Because your business is built on speculation, unlike the older generation advises — they are all set with their business ideas, they take the conventional path. But you, as the businessmen of today, want to take new challenges, you want to be innovative, you want to open up new areas of business. This innate desire to do something new or innovative is the sign of youthfulness. So you have the zeal and thirst to be different, but what plagues that spirit is the element of uncertainty or the fear of uncertainty. So, you need inner strength to combat this uncertainty, so that you can continue to be creative and relieve yourself from stress, and at the same time absorb wisdom from your elders and their experiences. We need to balance the four factors given below:

- Absorbing wisdom from our elders
- Maintaining our creativity
- Cope with uncertainty
- Free ourselves from stress, by learning how to handle it.

I recommend that you take a little time out for yourself and meditate regularly, recharge your batteries once every six months — a few days of reflection on the context of life. Not just seeing life in a box but seeing the bigger context of life. I assure you that it will give you enormous creativity, merit, inner strength and enthusiasm.

Human Touch in Human Resource
Excerpt from a talk by H. H. Sri Sri Ravi Shankar

I am glad to be here with all of you at this conference. When it comes to Human Resources, we need to have a human touch. A formal atmosphere is not congenial for authentic sharing. Apart from professional dealings, there needs to be an informal air as well at your workplace. So, I think in this conference we could practise that with just a little bit of informal getting to know each other, by saying "hello" to each other. Can you all greet the person sitting next to you, or behind you, or in front of you? Take 30 seconds to acquaint yourself with a person sitting near you and create an atmosphere, a sense of belongingness.

In India, all our scriptures begin with a question and there is a question and answer format. Now I want to ask you a question. Did you really get to know the person next to you a little or did you simply utter the usual greeting as a formality? Here lies the clue. Did you go beyond a formal "Hi. Hello. How are you?" I don't want you to answer. I know the answer. I don't want you to irritate the person sitting next to you. See, when you get off the aircraft, or when you leave a nice restaurant, the air hostess, or the staff or doorman at the restaurant smile at you and say mechanically, "Have a nice day." But they naturally don't mean it personally. Most of the pleasantries we exchange are at that level — a very dry sort of formality which does not touch the heart of a person in any way. The same words, "Be happy", "Have a nice day", when they come to you from a very dear friend, from your sister, brother, basically from one of your family members, it carries a certain sentiment, it brings some presence along with it, right? When we lose sight of this sentiment,   this presence of mind, when we miss authenticity in our communication with our colleagues, then the workplace becomes dry and dull. Motivation levels go down, there is no inspiration in the air whatsoever. And that is how we try to manage human resources without giving it a human touch. Does it work? It does not, it cannot. Because there's a difference between motivation and inspiration.

So what does it all mean? It means that you are so formal, you are walking around with a glass gaze all the time. It means we are content to remain in our shell and not really connect with one another, each time we communicate. As a result, there is no real communication, no bonding happening. We need to create that informal environment around us, wherever we go, for authenticity to blossom. We need to truly understand the difference between motivation and inspiration. What can we do for motivation — offer our employees a raise in pay, give them some bonus. Now this works for a couple of months maybe, and then that is it. It will not be enough to make the person's enthusiasm sustain over a longer period of time. But if people are inspired from within to take up a mission, to see a job through to successful completion, they will put their heart and soul into it and their efforts will bring success. This is what is needed then, this shift from motivation to inspiration. We see social activists and revolutionists going all out for a cause. We see them go to irrational extremes even, to fight for whatever they believe in. Can we somehow apply the same principle in our work environments and inspire people to take up a mission and achieve their goals? Think about why an entrepreneur would do a better job than an employee. It is not just about making more money. This is one of the salient questions we need to ask ourselves. Transforming the human mind is the key to driving success.

A sense of caring, compassion, a sense of belongingness — these are essential aspects of human growth, human relationships. Imagine this scenario. Someone is sick and is admitted in the hospital, and when you visit them, you ask them "How are you?" They reply, "I am fine." If they were fine, why are they in the hospital in the first place I say! But you see, our questions are many times quite irrelevant.

So if our communication remains at this superficial level, if we are this apathetic towards our fellow human beings, no wonder then that depression has become a common phenomenon in today's society. Today, a large chunk of the population in Europe is depressed. And now with the economy going down, the percentage of cases of depression must surely have gone up. Here, in our big cities too, the incidence of depression is visibly on the rise. Last week, I was in IIT Kharagpur. Do you know what the director told me? He said that the most frequently sold pharmaceutical drug in the campus is the antidepressant. Picture this — if people around you in the office are taking antidepressants, do you really expect them to deliver any better results in their work?

So we need to take care of not just our physical health, but also our mental health and emotional well-being. And I think that is the main reason why an HR department is created in every company, every business set up. Am I correct? The HR department is put in place precisely to deal with people's personal issues. But if people are being treated like machines, you do not need an HR department. HR is required to address all that we consider 'human'. So what are the qualities that we need to pay attention to then? Mental health, physical health, communication skills, the degree of inspiration or motivation that employees can hold on to and their capacity to take on work, and how to increase their capacity as they go. These are the issues one needs to reflect on. If you turn back time and look, 5100 years ago in the Bhagavad Gita, Lord Krishna did the same thing. He has been the first HR manager India knows. When Arjuna was so depressed and was not ready to do his job, Lord Krishna was with him in the battlefield, and told him all sorts of things. First, He warned Arjuna that people would blame him for sure. Then He incited Arjuna's ego and tried to wake him up. And then He offered His disciple different incentives, saying, "If you win, you will have the kingdom. If you lose, you will enjoy Heaven. Come on, fight." In many ways, Lord Krishna lifted Arjuna out of that depression.

So let us examine the doer now. There are three types of *karta*, or doer. One is the *sattvic* doer. What does the *sattvic* doer do?

Drutyutsahsamanvita — He is full of enthusiasm.

Sidhhyasidhhayo nirvikarah — Whether his efforts meet with success or not, he still learns something from the experience. With every failure he learns something, with every success too, he remains calm and moves on. He doesn't get bogged down by failures nor does he lose his humility when he finds success. That is the kind of abiding energy he comes up with. And he handles every situation to the best of his ability.

There there are the *tamasic* and *rajasic kartas*, or doers.

Dirghasutri — They say, "It is not possible."

In the case of some people, if you give them a project, they will come up with a hundred reasons for how it is not possible, how it will not work out. Then there are others who are always ready to take on challenges. And given the three types of *kartas*, knowing how to change from one to the other is all the methodology or technology that we need to make things work in any situation. So, from the *rajasic karta* or the *tamasic karta*, who is in slumber, who says "Nothing is possible" and "I can't do it," we go to "Ok, let's do it," "We have it in us. We will achieve it." Come up with brilliant ideas, innovate as much as you can, to manage any kind of situation at work. Determine to face every scenario with this kind of energy, so that transformation has to happen. You have titled this conference 'The Breath of Change' right? Breath definitely brings about the required change in us. Breath can change the doer, the person within you, the one who is depressed, angry, agitated, demotivated, into someone who is enthusiastic, creative, energetic, who is more cooperative and who can withstand any drawback, resolve any conflict.

Another issue that we need to look at is the way many people cannot stand criticism. I think this is a serious lapse in our education. We simply do not train people to withstand criticism. The moment someone criticizes us, suddenly we bring in a mental barrier. We shut down all levels of communication, become defensive and stop learning. I am of the opinion that if we can train people to take criticism and give constructive criticism when needed, then we will find such a huge difference in their attitude, in their behaviour, in their approach to any situation, and towards people as well. We need to inculcate an inclusive attitude, rather than encourage an attitude where we shut people out. The Art of Living has done many million human hours of workshops in the last couple of years. One lakh and fifty thousand workshops have been conducted in 2009 and 2010 alone. In all these workshops, what we have found is that it is possible to bring about immense change in human beings such that their productivity increases, their cooperation with their colleagues improves, their commitment to a job grows and their level of happiness is much greater. This is something that we need to really address — the happiness factor, creating an atmosphere of joy in the workplace. Sermons can be given but sermons really don't change our lives deeply. We need to instead teach them some very important techniques that they can apply at work. They need tools, they need methods, so that they can make the change happen on their own. This is why we built this foundation and we taught APEX programs on personal transformation. And it has really made a big difference in people's lives. Life cannot be compartmentalised — professional and personal aspects of life are not entirely separate. We have to see it in a holistic manner. So I would suggest that in your companies you should celebrate a family day. Maybe many of you already practise something of this kind. On this day, you ask people to come to work with their whole family, and create a certain sense of belonginess, a togetherness that goes beyond work.

30 years ago when we first carried out the programme in BHEL, I asked our teacher to ask some questions to the workers there. Some of the questions were, "Suppose you became the managing director of this company, what you would like to do? How you would like to see this company grow?" and "Have you ever thought that this company is the source of your livelihood?" "If this company flourishes then your job is secure. If this company goes down you cannot survive. Have you ever thought about it that way?" Many level-four workers do not even think this way. These people said, "We never thought like this. We thought it's just a job — come, take money, do whatever you can do and go back home." They had never felt that sense of belongingness, or thought about how they had put in hard work or how they could extract the rewards of their time and efforts. This new twist in their understanding made a lot of difference to their level of involvement

at work.

You may wonder why so many people come and participate in movements like Art of Living and other spiritual movements. Even if they get very little money for their work, or even if there's nothing offered, they still want to come and work. If you come to our Ashram, you will see that the housing department is the most stressful department to work in, because people suddenly turn up. 5,000 people land at our Ashram at one time and they all have different requirements — some want an Indian toilet, some want a Western one, some want double sharing in their rooms. And the housing team has to cater to all their needs. But you will be amazed — their smile never vanishes. Sometimes I have to tell them, "Go and rest now!" When I take a round at 11.30 in the night, they are still smiling and happy, eager to finish their work meticulously before they wind up for the day. And this type of enthusiasm only comes when the spirit is in its right place. And I do not mean the other type of spirit which we pass around in parties. This is the type of spirit which we kindle within the mind which makes working joyful. It is not that you work relentlessly and the results finally bring you some joy. The very process of work itself is happiness, it is joyful. And that can only happen when the individual transforms at a much deeper level of existence.

Q: What do we keep with us and what do we let go of, to be successful in this changing world?

Guruji: We retain our commitment and let go of our stress and bickering. In any work situation, bickering does arise, especially with those who have a very individualistic approach to things and those who are thinkers. If you think differently, you always find that some job could have been done better. And this bickering, this regret in the mind lingers and turns into complaint, becomes a point of frustration. I would say, let go of the frustration but keep your sense of commitment to the task at hand.

Q: What should be the approach of HR professionals today in managing generation Y?

Guruji: First of all, you should not feel that you are old. See yourself as a part of that young generation and sometimes, sit down and spend time with them. When you do not perceive yourself as old and when you have a level of involvement with them, they will start treating you as a part of their own clan. Once that communication gap is bridged, then there is no difficulty managing their issues.

Q: Guruji, you seem to suggest that the *sattvic guna* is somewhat better than the *tamasic* and the *rajasic*. I just wanted to hear your perspective on the immense strength and immense potential for human development that lies in *tamasic* or *rajasic* gunas.

Guruji: Firstly *tamasic guna* is lethargy, so there is no power that it brings. *Rajasic guna* has energy, has power, no doubt, but it is suited more to destroying a system rather than constructing it. If you want to do something very creative and constructive, then you need *sattvic gunas*. A little *rajasic* touch along with *sattva*, is also ok.

Q: Pranaam Guruji, how do we manage people with a negative attitude at the workplace?

Guruji: Send them to the Art of Living course. See, in one week you can find a metamorphosis — not even one week, rather in just 4 days. Once, one of the well known banks in India sent all their officers who were creating problems to the Ashram. There were 35 of them. I am talking about a time, some 7-8 years ago. Later on, they (the bank management) came to the Ashram and congratulated me. They said, "It was magic, nearly 90% of them became better!" Of course, there were a few who had been alcoholics for a long time. Though they had changed, it was not as drastic a change as the change the seniors saw in the others.

Chapter 6

Social Partnerships
Make Business Sense

We need to give people a vision.
Those who have a vision or
a dream can go ahead and develop society.

The health of a society today seems to be determined by the number of beds and cells available in hospitals and prisons. The prisons are filled and overflowing in many of the developed countries — prison occupancy today stands at 160%. They have to build new prisons in the so-called 'developed' countries. This does not denote a healthy society. A society where a significant percentage of the student population is jailed at least once, where one in five children consults a psychiatrist, is not a developed society.

So, the health of a society depends on the smooth functioning and availability of space in hospitals and prisons. We do not need to build more hospitals or prisons. We need to teach people how to be healthy.

Charity does not seem to be a part of the language of today. We have to build the self-esteem of people. Of course, we need to help them financially, but at the same time we have to make them aware of what they can do. We have to give them a vision. People who have a vision or a dream can go ahead and develop society. A person becomes motivated to do something either to fulfill a need or to realise a dream. However, we lack both. We are giving our people neither a vision nor a dream about our society, our world.

To give an example of how need motivates people to be pro-active, let us recall the earthquake in Gujarat, a time when everyone pitched in to help those affected. People gathered within two hours and prepared two thousand meals and shelters. That was to meet the urgency, the need of the hour. So, a calamitous situation, and the dire need it creates, makes people come forward and take initiative. Alternately, they should have a dream, a strong vision about their country, their state or their village.

When both these things are lacking, we will have a lukewarm, slow, under-developed economy. People in business have a dual role to play in society, like the Sun drawing water from the earth and giving it back in the form of rain. We are dependent on society and society in turn expects something from us. We need to think what about we can do for society. About what kind of society we want to leave behind for our children — one which is more beautiful than the one we inherited, or one which is more terror-stricken and fearsome, where there is a depletion of natural resources? These thoughts, this attitude of responsibility has to be ingrained in us and this can happen through education.

Rural India does not lack resources, it's just that they are misplaced. A white-collared employee earns less than a labourer does, in a village. But the labourer spends 60 percent of his income on liquor. Drug abuse and alcoholism are two key factors that drive poverty in our country. We need to address these issues.

A third factor is violence — domestic violence and violence

caused by stress, lack of understanding, and a narrow vision of life. So much is lost when violence takes over one's life, one's mind.

Success in any business is measured by the smile we have on our faces. The higher we go, the grimmer and stiffer we become. Most of our developments are hindered by this attitude of ours, this lack of communication. Improving communication, sensitivity towards the environment, a broader understanding about inter-dependence and a long term vision are the basic building blocks for sustainable development. Without these, our society would be like a stool without legs.

The media has an important role to play in our society. Unfortunately, we have a blame culture in this country. And we waste so much energy and time in playing this blame game. Whenever something goes wrong, we rush to point fingers at others. Of course, when there was disaster in Gujarat, the media was at a loss. They didn't know whom to blame. They couldn't blame the Government and they couldn't blame God because they don't believe in Him!

Our failure to take responsibility does not lead us anywhere. We cannot progress in society if we continue this way. We need to know that. Our main responsibility is to get people to be responsible, starting with taking responsibility for oneself. And that is what yoga is all about. Yoga means taking responsibility for your feelings, for your health, for the way things are in your life, and thereon, for the whole world. And I think this one principle can help nurture and sustain society in the long run.

Chapter 7

Environmental Management

All things that make up our environment
– the plants and the animals – are sacred.

Everything that exists on the planet is valuable. It is not just the spirit, but also the instrument through which the spirit manifests itself, that is important. Knowledge and money are sacred too.

It is human beings alone who pollute this planet. In a forest, there is no pollution. No animal ever causes pollution. No animal uses plastic. Birds know how to take care of the environment. Cats know how to keep their surroundings clean and pollution-free.

We have forgotten how to be this way because we have moved away from nature. We live in a mechanical, conceptual world rather than in the real world.

When we are tense and agitated, we pollute the environment by emitting vibrations which are not harmonious. Environmental damage is not caused by external objects alone, it is also a product of subtle factors within human nature. If we are in a room, feeling angry, agitated or depressed, anyone who enters the room will also feel depressed because the environment is charged with the vibes we give out. This is a big way in which we adversely affect our environment every day. A child may be upset and may cry or throw a tantrum, but the next minute he is happy and cheerful again. But when we are upset about something, it takes time for us to come back to our normal state of mind; sometimes even a week or a month! It takes us such a long time to smile and be cheerful with people around us again.

Thus we go around filling the environment with negative vibrations. Walk in a red light area or a drug peddling haven in a big city, it gives you such a heavy and horrible feeling. The atmosphere is so bleak that you want to run away from there. You just don't want to drive on such roads. Instead, when you drive through an area where there may be a school, or a temple or other place of worship, there is a distinct lightness, a certain positive energy you can instantly feel in the atmosphere. This is the difference in the effect of the vibrations we send out into the environment.

As we succeed in life, we become more rigid, more unfriendly and more strict. People wonder what happened to the friendly person of the past! As we grow in wealth and fame, we progressively harm the environment by spreading greed, anger and frustration around us.

The influence of the company you keep is indicated by your frame of mind after you consult them about your problems. After you have met and talked with them, do you go back feeling lighter, feeling that the problem does not really exist anymore, or do you feel heavier in your heart? The former indicates good company, the kind that has a positive effect on you; the latter shows company that needs much improvement.

If you have the ability to take everybody along with you and move forward, then you are preserving the pristine spiritual make up which we are all born with. Everyone is born with an inclination towards spirituality. As we grow, this trait gets lost somewhere. Our whole effort is to bring back that innocence, simplicity, joy and friendliness.

There are certain simple techniques by which you can come back to your natural state of being. Let us give it a name which everybody in the world can accept: Art of Living. There are basic principles of wisdom that you could follow to stay elevated, happy and enthusiastic.

Isn't it strange that we haven't taught our children how to be friendly with everybody? We harbour almost militant feelings towards other people. We are prepared to go to extremes even in day to day matters — we would rather die than drink water at somebody's house! If you harbour anger and hatred towards somebody, who do you think will lose? Revenge just chews you up. It destroys you before it destroys the other person. We need to learn how to get over our negative impulses and go back to being as pure as a child.

It is vital that we truly understand the connection between spirituality and the environment. Understanding cosmology is part of this connection. But as a society, somewhere along the way, we have got lost in consumerism. In earlier times, plates were made of leaves or similar bio-degradable material. Cups were also bio-degradable. So too were our pesticides, we used neem as a pesticide. We attached a certain sanctity to these things. We prayed to Shakti, the Mother Divine to keep us healthy, to destroy viruses and bacteria without polluting the environment.

But today, we do not seem to understand the damage we are causing our environment in the long run. Nowadays, people the world over are thinking about burying the dead. There will be little place left on the planet if we do this. Cremation is much better as it does not affect the environment. It will save our planet in many ways. In earlier times, in the Middle East, there was hardly any wood available, naturally, to light fires. This was because of the desert-like environment. So, they had to adopt the practise of burial. But now there are electric crematoriums which can be set up anywhere. We need to educate people about the rites they should opt for, irrespective of their religion.

Ultimately, we must make a distinction between spirituality and religion, as it applies even in our everyday lives. Religion is like a banana skin and spirituality is the banana. Spirituality is common to all religions. It is what keeps the enthusiasm, courage, confidence and the smile alive in our lives.

Chapter 8

Ethics and Business

*To follow ethics in business,
we need to be free from stress.*

L et us now examine ethics and business. Think about why
people generally pay attention to ethics. People follow ethics
out of fear — fear of losing their job, or fear of starvation, or fear
of prosecution. People also behave ethically out of a natural sense
of commitment to their work. Sometimes they may be tempted to
resort to unethical means in the false belief that they will benefit
more or gain favour with others. But that is not the case really,
when we see the broader picture. It is short term benefits and long
term problems that we get every time we follow unethical means.
It is best to always act on the right side of ethics. Though it may
feel tough initially or though you may find it difficult keeping
up your efforts in the long run, rest assured that it keeps up your
spirit, that it keeps you happy and healthy always. When people

realise the truth of this, their commitment to good ethics improves. What we have seen in our organisation the world over is a high level of motivation and commitment which springs out of innate happiness and not out of expectations, not out of saying, "OK, when you do this, you will find place in the heavens after your lifetime or you will find happiness in future." It comes from the right attitude that makes them ask of themselves — "How I can help people around me, how I can sustain this joy and happiness that I am experiencing right now?"

I see stress as the biggest problem. Stress and mistrust among colleagues within the organisation is a big hindrance to ethics. For a business to run based on sound ethics, you need to create an atmosphere of trust and caring, you need to develop a more human face to the business. Then this assurance, that by following the right ethics you will only go up the ladder in the organisation, has to come from the top. Do you know what we did? We conducted several 'Corporate Culture and Spirituality' programmes where we brought together big businesses, who have always practised ethics, who have practised certain corporate social responsibilities, and we got them to share their experience with the small businesses, as if to boost morale by saying, "See, if this big business could do so well, following a certain code of conduct and following good ethical practises, then you can also do that." This encouragement is what is needed today for every business, a sort of reassurance I would say, that you can walk on the right side of the ethics line and still make money. Often, people think that they can get away with a little bending of their ethics and make some quick and easy money, and they believe that will be able to sustain such actions. But that has proved to be an illusion in many cases including Enron and some dotcom companies. I do not want to mention names, but what I do want to emphasise here is that we need to instil faith in morality and faith in ethics at all levels in business. Think about it, no businessman wants his subordinates to cheat him. He would surely expect to see certain ethics in his workers, colleagues and subordinates. But for this expectation to percolate to their level, he has to practise those ethics himself, and that, I feel, is only possible when he is free from stress. We need to promote this mantra of being stress-free as much as we can, so that the workplace becomes more a place of celebration, a place of joy and happiness, with a feeling of commitment rather than tension, stress, mistrust among colleagues. Lately, I have often heard that people are not truly engaging in the work that they are doing; they are just working to make some money and then take off. It is not a healthy sign.

But you see the world over today, as I said earlier, the percentage of depression has risen alarmingly. In Europe, about one third of the population is depressed. I heard that in England, there is a big market for Prozac. If this trend continues, only a few companies will benefit, such as those manufacturing these pills; they will make big money no doubt, but people will suffer to no end. We need to look into the stress levels of people and think about how we can reduce these. And we need to devise many ways; there could be many ways in which the stress can be minimised or better handled and a sense of belongingness can be brought about in a workplace. With such efforts, the perception, observation and expression of people will change. And naturally, every enterprise, business or governmental office will show remarkable differences in their results. We have seen this take place in many cases. So, I would say that, for every employer, just giving a raise or increment to a person in service is not enough; you need to see that your employees are always in a good mood, in a healthy environment that motivates and challenges them. And it is possible for every business to create such an atmosphere, such an environment.

Now in an NGO, this is even more difficult. Do you know why? Because you do not pay them but you expect them to do the work. When you are not paying and they have to work, they are their own bosses; nobody can tell them what they should be doing or how they should go about achieving their goals. You can only give broad guidelines. But what really makes a person work? Whether it has been a flood or a tsunami situation, I only get the reports later. I do not even have to tell them that they have to go and work there. People come with such a high level of motivation. They get together and say, "Hey there has been a disaster, we have to immediately rush to help out." And so when there was a disaster in Surat, about 5 lakh people volunteered just like that. No governmental machinery could match the work that these volunteers did together. And what makes all these good people come together and work so hard for a cause is just a sense of commitment, the compassion they carry in their heart. They are people who bring in the human touch. If we lose this human touch in business, I do not think any business can sustain for too long. To bring out that human touch should be a priority in today's stressful world. Ethics in business will bring about trust, will bring about productivity, and will ultimately make the business grow better. Today, if you see the daily newspapers and the television channels, you are bombarded with negative news all the time and people only get more and more depressed. We need to bring people out of such depression as depression will not help business at all! We need to encourage all those who have practised business ethically to share their experience with others so that such models become popular.

I would like to share with you an interesting event that we faced. Our international centre in the outskirts of Bangalore is surrounded by villages — there are about 20 villages in the vicinity. A few years ago, I gathered the villagers, all unemployed youths — about 500 of them. And I called the Minister for Small-Scale Industries and asked him to present to the villagers all the various schemes they could avail of. So here was a government with money and schemes at their disposal, and on the other side, there were people who were unemployed. As I saw it, why not bring them together and let them work, to see if they could do something in coordination. When the Minister presented all the projects that they had on hand and assured the gathering that they would be paid for the work they did, and that they were willing to provide the resources the villagers would need to develop their ideas, these 500 youths remained negative about how each one of those ideas would not work, how none of those projects would actually take off. Finally, what they wanted was a government job — some wanted jobs in the police and some wanted jobs as drivers or conductors. It was so amazing to see such a low level of motivation in people to take up a business opportunity and work towards it, their complete lack of interest in working hard to get where they want. If people are poor in the world today, I say it is to some extent because of their lethargy, because either they want to make easy money or they just want to live on charity. In the end, the same youngsters started the Youth Leadership Training Programme, we got them to do some exercises and breathing and meditation. I tell you, that very group came up with ideas, they started their own businesses and became entrepreneurs. Many of them are doing so well today that they could run charities of their own, in just five years! For unemployed youth to become good businessmen in five years is very tough, but it is possible and it has happened only because of that motivation, that inspiration they found within themselves. They could finally get up and get moving with a commitment to doing something to improve their lives, rather than pointing fingers at the government. We need to undertake more of these motivational and inspirational programmes, whether in Ethiopia or Kenya or India or Nepal. I believe our youth do need such de-stressing, de-lethargising programmes. And I would like you all to please consider this — if you all get together once or twice a year to spread the message among people in your area, in your community, in your circle of acquaintances and friends, that you can run a business perfectly ethically and still bring prosperity and progress to society, that would build and boost morale for so many businesses, small and big, around the world.

In the absence of ethics, politics would be clogged with corruption, business with greed and religion with terrorism. We need to work towards eliminating these negative outcomes, and to do that, we need to focus on values. So as I see it, there are three things we need to do:

- Spiritualise politics

- Socialise business (business will have to take on social responsibility, those in business will need to care for the society)

- Secularise religion

We need to adopt these long term goals, and nurture the long term vision needed to fulfill them. Values and ethics will provide that vision. It is mostly greed and economic reasons that make people stray from their innate values. If we can reassure people in society that we are here to support them, to help them live by their values, I think we will have a more beautiful world, a more free world, and not just a free world, but a fair world.

Guruji answering some questions

What is your take on competition? I compete with my siblings for the attention of my parents. I compete with my fellow students for getting the grades I want. At every stage of my life I am competing, and today, in this environment, that brings on a lot of stress, and probably also the pressure to resort to unethical methods along the way. What do you advise? Do you have a mantra which can tell me, "This is good, you should compete with it"?

You know, you should compete with yourself. This is the healthiest thing you can do. The very fact that you want to compete means you are not very confident about your abilities. Only when you look outside yourself, when you have your eye on someone else, can you begin to compare. But if you are centred and you know your abilities, you involve yourself wholly in the task at hand, unmindful of who are around you and what they are doing. Think about the Wright brothers and what they gave the world! They did not have competition. They did not try to look at anybody else wanting to compete. If you are creative, you do not need to bother about competition. You only have to enhance your own creativity. Then, if at all you want to compete, you should compete with yourself — see how well you did last year, how much more you want to do this year. That is my view. It is almost like the running race — when you run, you should not look to your sides. If you do, trying to see who is running faster, then you will lose the race. Your eye should be focused only on your track and you should give it your 100%. And then you will see that whether you win or lose, you are happy.

I compete because I want attention and I want to be accepted, I want to become a part of their group or become one with them. And I am just looking at my thing, it's "me" and always "me" but my parents taught me that "me" is not the right way. It should be "us" or "we". How can I become a part of "we"?

Sometimes, the more you want to become a part of somebody else, the more easily everybody will notice that there is some artificiality in you. You need to tell yourself that certain things are a given. You are a part of the universe, whether you are intelligent or not, you are a part of the society and you should be confident in the knowledge that they all accept you. Your wanting approval or acceptance from somebody puts you in a certain amount of tension which nobody else is able to take away from you. You should just relax. Take it for granted that you are one among them and behave that way. Do you see what I am saying? Otherwise, you become too self-conscious, and when you are so self-conscious, you are bound to make mistakes.

Some of your followers are also industrialists. Does their code of ethics rub off on their family lives too or are they ethical only in their business? How do these people interact or deal with their own problems?

You know, people thrive on problems. If there is none, they create one because they are so used to living with problems! Having created a problem, they should know how to solve it too. That is what we tell them, "Hey, look, you have created a problem. Now learn to solve it on your own because nobody else can come and solve it for you." I would not say that all these business groups or industrialists are free from problems or that they have solved all their problems at once. They may be facing many problems which they do not even discuss with others. But one thing is for sure, they know how to handle their emotions, how to balance their mind, how to be more reasonable in their dealings with other people.

Reason must always take the front seat. Often, what happens while facing problems is that reason takes a back seat, emotion takes the front seat and that is when the ruin begins. It ruins everything. If reason dominates emotions, then in the long run, people benefit. And many of these businessmen have experienced this in reality, and that is why they wanted all the workers in their setup, in their business, to be taught the same lesson.

Chapter 9

Combating Corruption

The big 'C' of corruption can be countered by five other 'C's. Let us look at these other 'C's.

Connectedness

A lack of connectedness or sense of belonging breeds corruption in the society. That is why people often look to form connections, to avoid corruption. That explains why corruption is at its lowest in the villages and much greater in the cities where there is, at best, a poor sense of community and minimal interaction between people. Creating this sense of belonging is one of the greatest ethical challenges we face as a society. Corruption cannot be rooted out without this bonding.

Today, we do not believe in investing in friendship. We only believe in investing in currency notes. Our security has shifted from friendship to currency. Half a century ago, a person would feel very secure when he had a lot of friends. Friends were his constant social support system, so he was not easily corruptible. He did not depend on just a few bills to get by. He said to himself, "There are people around me who are going to help me out." Today, due to a lack of connectedness, you fear whether your own children are going to care for you or not. Because of this sense of isolation everywhere, the only feeling of security you find is in telling yourself, "Ok, amass more wealth," and you keep it all in your personal account. Money has become the sole source of security. This is not just an individual phenomenon or way of thinking. It has become a collective phenomenon.

Naturally, corruption is on the rise because we do not feel connected with people around us. Basic human values such as spirituality, brotherhood, friendliness, compassion — all these have either decreased, or in some cases, dissolved entirely. So the only thing that is there with us any longer is money, money and more money.

Courage

Another reason for corruption is a lack of self-esteem and confidence in one's own abilities. Corruption can be minimised when a person finds a sense of stability and safety in his own abilities and self-confidence. It's the fear and insecurity in people which makes them more susceptible to corruption. And then they try to find security in money and this does not really work, as we discussed above. They do acquire more money but the sense of insecurity stays on. In fact, they now become more frightened and shaky because all that money would not have been earned in the right manner. We must focus on creating courage in a person, courage and confidence in his abilities and skills, and in the laws of nature.

Cosmology

An understanding of cosmology is essential — looking at one's own life in the context of extended space and time. A human life span of 80-100 years is so short in the context of the billions of years that have passed since creation. Scientists estimate that the earth is 15 billion years old. Everything in this creation is recycled. The air we breathe is old. Every cell in our body is old. The oxygen and hydrogen available is old and this cycle will continue. Seeing life in the context of our vast universe and the limitlessness of time will deepen one's perception of life and broaden one's vision and mind. It is sure to enrich one's heart.

Care and Compassion

These virtues can infuse more dedication into society. A lack of dedication sows the seeds of corruption. To give you an example, in 2001, there was a huge spiritual gathering in India where 30 million people participated. On one particular day, there were 3 million people gathered in one place. And there was not a single robbery or act of violence. People were staying in tents and mingling with each other, but no crime occurred.

It was January and bitterly cold. I went to volunteer, to take care of the people gathered there, some of whom were very poor and could not bear the cold, as they had come from warmer climates. At midnight, the volunteers were distributing blankets. The temperature was close to zero degree Celsius. They offered a blanket to a certain young man in his 20s. But he declined it and said that it could be given to some elderly women who stood nearby instead. He assured us that he could handle the cold. That's the kind of compassion I am talking about. That kind of care, compassion and understanding that somebody else may be needier than us, can help us root out corruption.

When there is a sense of community, especially inspired by a spiritual cause, crime rates come down drastically. Somebody asked me, "Guruji, please address the basic issue of corruption. We are forced to bribe people; if we do not bribe some people, our industries suffer. This is the sad but unavoidable condition here in India.What do we do?"

If you can bridge your company with the society around you, you have the support of this society that you are a part of. You can minimise these hostile conditions to a great extent with your inclusive attitude. Social responsibility should be an essential part of our corporate culture.

Commitment

An individual sense of commitment to contributing to society is essential to combat corruption. When a person has a goal and a commitment to a higher cause in life, then there is a shift from receiving to giving. In a society, if everyone keeps thinking about what they will gain rather than what they can contribute and how they can be useful to people around, then corruption cannot be rooted out.

A few years ago, there was an earthquake in Gujarat. An elderly lady lost her entire family. One of our Swamijis who had gone to be of service at the time, met this lady. She wanted to donate 10 rupees. He told her that he had gone there only to give and not to take. But the lady replied that she had lost everything and her sense of giving should not be taken away too.

The sense of contributing to society has to be re-awakened among us. And this is impossible without individual spiritual growth and a personal sense of belonging to the whole world. The globe has become a village. We have globalised everything except wisdom and I think this is one of the causes of terrorism and unrest in the world today. We accept food and music from every part of the world, but when it comes to wisdom we shy away. If every child on the planet learns a little bit about all the different cultures and values, (religious, moral and spiritual) the whole scenario will be different. A lack of this kind of education has caused too many problems in the world.

One of my teachers was the personal secretary to Mahatma Gandhi. When we were young, he would tell us stories of his life and of how Mahatma Gandhi inspired people to do selfless service by his own example. That impression stayed with us children for a very long time, that sense of commitment to service and the feeling of belonging to everybody.

We can create these feelings through our own example. I think all religious leaders, business establishments, political establishments, social workers and NGOs around the world should come forward and bring out this message of unity. We are not living in compartments anymore. The world has become one family.

Management Mantras

Chapter 10

Management and Meditation

For a good manager, it is important to be in the
present moment with patience and poise!

If you are intelligent, you may not be able to bear the lack of intelligence in others. The management profession requires dealing with diverse situations and people. To be able to deal with them justly requires a sharp intellect, patience, endurance and presence of mind.

How can we develop patience?

We have never been taught how to handle our mind. The tendency of the mind to be in the present moment needs to be cultivated and nurtured, so that one can develop patience and sharpness. This can be done by attending to one's breath and by meditating. Breathing exercises help in improving our perception, observation and expression and this is vital for good management.

Every time you expect some perfection in others' speech or action, you should take care not to lose the balance or perfection of your own mind and to pay close attention to your own inner feelings.

The Mind

We have never taken a close look at our minds. The faculty with which we hear and see is the mind. When you listen to someone, you may continually agree or disagree with what is being said. It is your intellect which is doing this. And you remember what is being said because of your memory.

There are seven levels to our existence: body, breath, mind, memory, intellect, ego and self. When we get to know a little bit about each of these layers, there is a transformation.

The sign of true success is the ability to smile at all times. You are successful when you are compassionate, cultured and committed. Education needs to provide all these values. We should not see all these values as goals to be achieved in the next 5-10 years of our life, or in the next life.

Let us examine the mind for a moment. Suppose you want me to tell you something about management. And I tell you to go to a library where you will find hundreds of books on the topic. Suppose I tell you that I am not a professor and have not gone to any management school. When you hear this, what will be your reaction? What will happen in your mind? There will be a state of waiting. Waiting can lead to frustration or to meditation. When you are not waiting, your mind is usually racing with thoughts. When your mind is waiting, your mind is stationary.

Are you aware of what goes on in your mind when you interact with people — the inner dialogue you have with yourself? Being aware of this is very important and helps to keep you healthy.

We need to look closely at ourselves, our lives and the roles we are playing at any given time.

What we expect of others rarely matches how we behave in their situation. Let me give you a simple everyday example. You will not be totally comfortable when you are a guest in somebody's house. You will tend to feel inhibited and uncomfortable. But when you have guests coming over to your house, you will not want them to feel uncomfortable. You will want them to feel at home and be in complete harmony with their surroundings. Yet you will not feel the same way at somebody else's place! Have you ever thought about this before? Why do we see ourselves differently from the way we see others?

Time for Reflection
We all need time for reflection. I think every human being needs to sit back for a little while and find that inner peace; everyday if possible. When our mind is agitated or restless and when we are too active, we are not tapping the source that lies deep within us. That source is our intuition. It gives us correct thoughts and confidence. So a few minutes of silence, a few minutes of reflecting on the truth, on our lives, would be extremely beneficial. We need the clarity and awareness it brings.

What are the ways and means to achieve that inner peace? We need to find an answer for this basic question that crowds our hearts and minds.

Observing that everything is changing, in our world, in our lives, in our society, will give us a clue that there is something that remains unchanged. The reference point, by which we observe that things are changing, is something that is not changing in itself. And this non-changing aspect of our consciousness gives us enormous strength, courage and creativity. A few minutes of experiencing that still aspect, deep within us all, energises our body, focuses our mind, frees our intellect from inhibitions, frees our memory from trauma and gives a joyful flavour to our disposition. We are able to get in touch with the joy that we are seeking.

It is not just enough to be able to experience responsibility or peace within us. We need to bring it out in the open in our society. This can only be done by educating people in human values, by rejuvenating human values in society.

A school or college student will usually have only 4-5 friends. If they cannot be friendly with the 30-40 kids in their classrooms, how are they going to be friendly with the 6 billion people in the world? Basic values such as friendliness, compassion, understanding and harmony in diversity need to be cultivated in schools, colleges and in every environment that an individual is exposed to.

Love is the very central force of human life and it overshadows all our stress. So the spiritual knowledge or education contained in human values will help an individual stand up to the demands of the day and help him manage all the problems he faces in daily life.

Man is at a crossroads today. Burdened by his many problems, he becomes violent or frustrated or he feels depressed or suicidal. Knowledge about our inner spirit can bring freedom from this frustration and violence. The spirit is all about love, beauty and peace. It transcends the boundaries of our acquired concepts, our imagination and our identities.

A violence-free society, a disease-free body, a quiver-free breath, an-inhibition free intellect and a trauma-free memory — these are the birth right of every individual. And as responsible citizens, we need to make our society and its component communities take this seriously. We need to make every individual take responsibility for himself and for the environment around.

Faculties of Existence

We look at everything outside us but we ignore our own faculties. Just as there are various faculties for various departments in companies and institutions, so too are there many faculties we possess in life.

The first faculty is the body. You become aware of your body only when it aches. Did you know that pain is basically your body asking for attention? At home, a child throws tantrums when he is not given attention. Your body behaves in a similar manner, it wouldn't throw tantrums if you paid regular attention to it. Being aware of your body is a good thing. And this is not just about food and exercise.

Ancient people called this awareness Yoga Nidra. To practise it, you need to lie down and turn your attention to each part of your body and regard it with love. No doubt, you may do it unconsciously, but doing it consciously is different. The closest thing to you is your body. It is the first layer of your existence.

The second faculty is the breath. The breath is what makes the distinction between say, leather and skin. When you are not breathing, your body has no value. It is this breath which gives you life. When we came into the world, the first act of our life was to take a breath, and then we cried. The last act of our life will be to breathe out and make others cry. But we ignore this primordial function in our life. Our breath contains many secrets. Every emotion has a corresponding rhythm in your breath. If you attend to your breath, your emotional disturbances can be removed.

The third faculty is our mind, through which we perceive, see and taste. Say there are some sounds in the background reaching your eardrums but your mind is elsewhere, you will not be able to hear these sounds. We know very little about our mind. If you are paid 10 compliments and insulted once, what will you remember? The 10 compliments will fly away and you will treasure the one insult. Our memory functions in a very funny manner. Your memory will hold on very tightly to anything that is of interest to you. You will always absorb something if you are deeply interested in it. If you love astronomy, it will be easy to remember the various details involved, which others may find very trying.

The fourth faculty is intellect. You continually form opinions on what you see or hear. Something is happening in you, some sort of analysis and judgement — accepting, not accepting, questioning etc. All this is due to this particular faculty that is ever active in us.

The fifth faculty is ego. You are caught up in your ego trips so often. When you are happy, something in you expands. Ego brings with it happiness, creativity, shyness and sadness. If you are shy and timid, it is because of your ego. Joy and pride too are an outcome of ego and so too, is sadness. There is ego behind every tear we shed. We know very little about the function of the ego in our lives. But just imagine, a little knowledge about it would make us so strong! We wouldn't be so vulnerable then.

The sixth faculty is something that is perhaps not so clear to you. Sometimes, when you are very relaxed or when you are in love, you feel that there is more to life than what you see. You sense that there is something more mysterious at play. It may happen when you are watching the sky, or reading the Gita, or watching TV, or taking a shower, or when you are sick with fever, or when a baby is born, or when you have fainted. That faculty is self consciousness or the *Atma*.

Sometimes, when you see young people, you feel as if you alone have not grown up while everyone else around you has. You feel as if you have not changed but everything else around you has. This feeling is so precious. Unfortunately, you let it slip away and hardly take any notice of it. Those few seconds would have given you so much peace and tranquillity. Meditation is a conscious experience of that aspect within you that enriches the other six layers.

Neither at home nor at school has anybody ever taught you how to deal with your mind and your emotions, or how to come out of the state of being depressed, angry, jealous or tense.

Nobody taught Thomas Edison how to make a light bulb. He did it on his own. If you learn something yourself, it feels great. Nobody taught me the Art of Living course. But you should always be open to learning. If you don't learn from your own intuition, you should take advantage of someone else's intuition.

Yoga and the Breath

Our breath can play a vital role in cleansing us of our negative emotions. We have experimented with this and tested it in many prisons around the world. 120,000 prisoners around the world practised a few breathing exercises and they were able to get rid of the hatred, anger and vengeance that clogged their minds and hearts. Within every culprit is a victim crying out for help. It is stress, the lack of a broad outlook on life, a lack of understanding and bad communication that foster violence in society.

If we observe a baby, we will find that from the time of birth until the age of three, it does a lot of exercises; exercises which we, as adults, don't do. In fact, a baby does a lot of yoga exercises. If you closely follow what a baby does, then you won't even need a yoga teacher.

Each of us has practised yoga as a baby. For instance, one of the things that a baby does is to lie down on its tummy and lift its legs up. Then, it puts one hand on the floor and raises the other hand. Yoga has developed like that.

Yoga means making you child-like, full of enthusiasm, joy and a sense of belonging with everybody.

The way a child breathes is very different from the way adults breathe. Our breath is linked to our emotions. We may be upset, unhappy or agitated and may want to get rid of these feelings. But we may not know how to do it. And it is in such a situation that our breath offers us a most precious secret. We can get rid of such negative emotions by understanding a few patterns and rhythms of breath. Then, we will have a good amount of control over how we feel.

Often, we say that we feel bad as though we are a victim of our feelings, as though we can't do anything about our feelings and emotions. But our breath gives us the secret to handle them, whether they are anger, frustration, fatigue or stress. We can change, in 5-10 minutes, any tendencies which are not life-supporting, by changing our own breathing pattern.

The Art of Living has been very successful in this respect. And these practises are being taught the world over. Currently, 27% percent of Europe is reeling under depression. I was given this statistic a couple of years ago at a meeting of the Psychologists' Congress of Europe in Athens, Greece, which I was invited to address. And they had projected that in the next eight years, this figure could go up to 48%. They exclaimed that they could not possibly give Prozac to the entire population! And even if they did, its effectiveness would decline with greater usage. Then they would have to look for alternative solutions. They wanted to see the research that we had done at the All India Institute of Medical Sciences and the All India Mental Health and Neuro-Sciences Institute of the Government of India.

This research showed that the breathing exercise of *sudarshan kriya* and *pranayama* could eliminate depression, mental tension and stress.

Millions of people have been relieved by these techniques. Science has also authenticated it with systematic research. Learning about our breath can help us in many ways.

Ultimately, it helps in making society crime-free and violence-free. When the prisoners learn these techniques, they wonder why these were not taught earlier. For perhaps, they would never have done anything wrong and been imprisoned in the first place!

The ultimate outcome of applying these techniques is a crime-free society, a disease-free body and a quiver-free breath. You may have noticed that your breath becomes very shaky sometimes. Many of our problems manifest through irregular breathing patterns. The mind is often inhibited. It has an opinion, an image about somebody. But then it changes. And many times we are not even aware of how fast it changes. You may notice that your opinions about people change all the time, sometimes even in a matter of a few minutes!

An intellect free of inhibitions and a memory free of any kind of trauma — these are the birthright of every individual in society. We all want a violence-free society. There is so much street violence around the world. The perpetrators of this violence need help. Every culprit is a victim too, and if you heal such people and teach them to manage their anger and aggression, they will understand things better. They will become positively dynamic and channelise themselves better.

When we practise breathing exercises and *sudarshan kriya,* our immune cells multiply many times, making us far less prone to disease. Again, this is scientific research I am speaking about.

A healthy person in a healthy society will be able to achieve all these goals — a disease-free body, a quiver-free breath, a confusion-free mind, an inhibition-free intellect, a trauma-free memory and a sorrow-free soul. But we all have to unite and see how we can bring this about.

Today, our society is beset with issues of violence and terrorism and this is because we have not globalised wisdom. When a child grows up thinking that people following his religion alone will go to heaven and everybody else will go to hell, then that child is going to create a big problem for everybody when he grows up! Instead if every child is educated in an atmosphere of acceptance then he will never grow up to endorse terrorism. He would never come to be a narrow-minded, fanatical fundamentalist.

One-World Family

Think of everyone around you as a member of the same family. They may be of a different religion, race, culture or nationality. It does not matter. They are all a part of you, a part of your own family. This broad vision needs to be promoted in the world today.

What is needed most is that we respect and honour each other.

We live in a global village; even if a small part of the globe is left behind in darkness, the world is not a safe place. We accept food from every part of the world. We eat Danish cookies and Chinese food. People everywhere listen to all sorts of music. The technology we use is completely globalised. Even our clothes reflect this global culture. In the same way, we must globalise our wisdom. I feel there is a strong need for this. We don't become Chinese just by eating Chinese food. In the same way, we don't become Indian just by practicing yoga or meditation.

All knowledge that is available in the world belongs to everybody, is common to the whole world. Mankind needs to be seen as one global society. It is when this is lacking that there is war, stress and all sorts of tensions.

Chapter 11

The ABC of Life

Awareness, Belongingness. Commitment –
the ABC of life – can enhance human values
amongst us today.

W hat is the ABC of life? It is Awareness, Belongingness and Commitment. These are the three, most vital pre-requisites to progress in any field. Today, we need them most in business and industry. Let us understand these, starting from the outermost or universal, moving inwards to the individual or personal.

The first essential is an awareness of sustainable development. We cannot espouse too much consumerism, be too greedy and destroy our planet. We need to hone our awareness on various levels — environmental awareness, awareness of human values, awareness of ethics in our business and awareness of how to achieve sustained development of our planet. And along with this awareness, comes the second requisite — a sense of belongingness.

To run a corporation, we need a sense of belongingness

that binds its people together. You will see that the success of an institution depends to a great extent on the degree of belongingness among its people. When people go beyond thinking in terms of "I" and view problems and situations collectively, they are better able to find solutions. So, do we create a sense of belongingness in people around us? This is an all-important question we need to ask of ourselves.

The third factor contributing to progress would be a sense of commitment. Of course, where A and B are found, C naturally follows. And if it does not, then we only need to give more encouragement and time for that to happen. Once these three things are in place, D or direction plays a role, enabling us to give a worthwhile direction to our lives.

Are you all here 100%? Do you notice that as I am speaking, you are most likely saying "yes" or "no" in your own mind? This is where awareness comes in. Are we aware of what we are telling ourselves? The important thing is not whether it is a yes or a no, but whether we are conscious of what the mind is saying to itself? This level of awareness alone creates a big transformation in the society, because in this state of mind, with this kind of alertness, a crime cannot take place. It becomes almost impossible for a criminal to do what he otherwise may, if he exercises this extent of awareness.

I would like to tell you a story about a saint. A thief once came to a saint and said, "See, I can't stop stealing. I am a pathological stealer. What do I do?" The saint said, "Look, I'm not going to tell you not to steal, but I am going to advise you to steal with awareness. Whenever you try to steal something, first look at your hand and know what it is going to do, and then with that awareness, go steal something." The man came back to meet the saint after three months, and said, "Swamiji, it was impossible! I could not steal with awareness"

The same happens with anger. Anger comes as a sudden

outburst, as we commonly say, "I lost it." What is it that you lost? Nothing but awareness. To do something destructive, all you need is momentary passion, an impulse. You can evoke passion in a person and he can go and destroy something. But to do something creative, we need more than passion. What we need is awareness. We need a certain focus. Often we do a lot to bring out the passion in people around us but very little to improve the level of awareness.

How can we increase awareness? There are simple things you need to observe and practise — take some time out to do very simple things in life, sometimes seemingly insignificant things, such as star-gazing, bird-watching, watching the sunrise or sunset, taking a walk, silently observing your breath. These are a few examples of simple exercises that we can easily follow to develop our awareness. Even in an everyday act such as eating food, you can inculcate awareness by eating slowly, paying attention to the smells and colours in the food and tasting everything you eat.

Awareness nurtures the intellect, belongingness nurtures the heart and commitment ultimately nurtures our life on the whole. So, even if a few people in society can create that sense of commitment in everybody around them, a lot of good work can be done. Just think about it, people who create problems are very few but they do it with such commitment that they manage to come up with really serious problems!

If we could look around us and think — "All the people on this planet belong to me" — I believe that is the moment our spiritual journey begins. Spirituality is simply the belongingness we feel with the entire universe.

Have you ever thought about the fact that you have landed on this planet a few years ago — 20, 40, 60 years ago — and you are going to be here for only a few more decades? Is this awareness lingering somewhere at the back of your mind? If it is, I tell you, you will be out of your depression in no time, you will be rid of your misery, of all your sorrow. See life in the context of cosmology. The vastness of space and time deepens our awareness, it elevates us.

There is an old tradition in India, one that is practised even today. People go to any temple and do what is called *sankalpa*. *Sankalpa* is remembering how old this universe is — several billion years old. Then they say — "In all these years gone by, on this day in this Kali Yuga, in this particular year, in this particular month, at this particular time, at this moment, I have this desire. God, please fulfill this." Cosmology heightens awareness and this awareness eliminates so many vices in life.

Another method adopted to create that awareness is meditation, *pranayama,* deep breathing. What is the first act we performed when we were born? We breathed in deeply and then we started crying. And do you know what the last act is? We breathe out and make everybody else cry. But in between these first and last breaths, we seldom address our breath, we seldom observe our breath. Our breath has great secrets to offer. It can show us how vast our mind is, how resourceful our consciousness is. This understanding of the power of our breath along with what I call cosmology, that is seeing life in the context of space and time, can make a big difference to the quality of our lives.

So you see, A stands for Awareness, B for Being and Belongingness, C for Cosmology, Commitment and Compassion — these are fundamental factors that can enhance human values amongst us today.

One last thing we do not realise the importance of... Smiling. We need to smile more often in life. A little bit of humour can keep us out of trouble. A few minutes of joy, a few smiles to ourselves every day. Do you know that when you are upset or angry, if you just look into the mirror, most of your negative emotions will disappear? Have you ever tried this? Suppose you are angry, let someone come and hold a mirror in front of you, I bet you cannot hold your anger, you just cannot. There is a tradition people follow in Karnataka — when a guest comes home, the women come with a *kalash* and a mirror held in front of it. In Maharashtra too, they do it. You are looking into yourself. When you look at me, you are not looking at me, you are looking at yourself. If you are afraid, you think I am a source of terror for you; if you have misery in your heart, you feel I am going to harm you; if you have love in you, you will see that in me too. If you look into the mirror, your anger, your greed, your lust, all these negative emotions which bother you will just dissolve and disappear. So, looking into the mirror every day and smiling is something vital, but we do not understand this really. We rarely smile. Sometimes, you are afraid that if you smile, somebody might take advantage of you. There is no point living life like that. I measure success by the smile a person has. How strong or how fragile your smile is indicates how successful you are in your life, in your business, how secure and confident you feel as a person, and that indicates the success of your career too.

Questions and Answers

In this final chapter, the author, His Holiness Sri Sri Ravi Shankar, answers questions from believers and sceptics alike.

Guruji, there is a smile that comes from the inner being and then there is also a smile that is given just to impress people. How do I smile all the time?

There is a saying in America, "Fake it till you make it." See, you have smiled often as a child, it came naturally to you, but somehow now that has changed. Never mind even if it is artificial, just develop the habit of smiling every now and then and you will see that as an extension of the habit, you frown less often. When you frown, you use up 72 muscles and nerves. When you smile though, you use only 4. Even economically you see, it is a good idea — not to waste your energy frowning. So, for a few minutes every day, if you take time out for yourself to breathe deeply and observe your breath, you can bring such relaxation, both to the body and to the mind. You may still feel boredom by afternoon, say by 3 or 4 o'clock. Now you know why I do not give any talks in the afternoon after lunch, when I feel sleepy and sometimes doze off. So you see all this talk is not meant to incite your passions, you were meant to sleep anyway!

But if you do some breathing exercises or meditation, just a few minutes of it energises your whole system. This is precisely what has happened in about 175-180 companies here in India. When they practise meditation at the end of the day, people feel as if they have suddenly come to life now, so that when they go back home, not so tired or completely worn out, they are able to spend time with their spouse and children, they are able to stay up to watch television till 10 o'clock. There are people who work all day in factories, and when they go home in the evening, they are half-dead. They are ready to just eat and jump into bed. You need energy, and that energy will come not just from food and sleep, but also through deep meditation, in a silent state of consciousness.

These exercises help us to concentrate and calm our minds. But could you elaborate on darshan *or meeting with God or* moksha.
Yes, definitely. God has no escape. See, God is love; God is that energy which is all-pervading. I will tell you a short story. A small boy, about eight years old, asked his father, "Dad, tell me, what is God? What does God look like?" The father takes the child by the hand and asks him, "Do you see the sky, can you see the space?"

The boy says, "Yes."

The father replies, "God is like that."

There is no escape from space. Everything exists in space, is born in space and will ultimately dissolve in space, but to feel that space within you, you need to relax a little, and you must go deep into meditation. So, first be human, and then from humanness, go on to Godliness.

How does one smile? From the moment you wake up till you go back to bed at night, there are problems surrounding you on all sides. How does one smile through it all?

Yes. If you only focus on the problem, you cannot smile. But the one who is going to solve the problem is right there in the mirror and is much more powerful than the problem, know that and you can keep smiling.

Yes, I agree, to get rid of those problems, I chant the Gayatri mantra facing the sun. That act for that moment gives me some relief but what about the rest of the time? How will my problems vanish? I cannot meditate all the time!

Yes, you are right. You do not need to meditate all the time; just as you do not take a shower all day long. Do you stand in the shower the entire day? No. You take a shower twice a day, once in the morning and maybe once in the evening, and if it is summer and you really need it, maybe three times a day. But that is good enough. In the same way, when you look at the problem you should also know that it is getting solved. Something appears to be a problem because you think you cannot handle it but when you see that there is potential in you that is bigger than the problem... it will cease to be a problem! So many problems have come to so many people on this planet and they have overcome them all, so will it happen with this one too. We have overcome World Wars, we have tided over economic and other crises. The spiritual strength you have within you is something that can lift you from your depression and sorrow. Today, it is not the poor who are committing suicide. I tell you, the majority of suicides are taking place among well-educated and capable people. They feel a certain emptiness in their lives, something lacking within themselves. It is not enough that we cater to the food and clothing needs of people; we need to nurture their soul, their inner being. And do not think that spirituality is only for the rich or only for the poor. For the rich, it opens their heart and for the poor, it gives them self-confidence. So, it is equally necessary for both.

What is the relationship between business and spirituality?
Many businessmen think spirituality is against economic prosperity and not beneficial to business. The benefits of the practise of yoga and meditation for business are:

- It increases energy and enthusiasm levels at the workplace
- It helps in time management and in maintaining a work-life balance
- It enhances alertness and awareness

Authentic leadership, creativity and smooth operations in any business require alertness and awareness of the present moment. Practise of yoga and meditation will help in achieving these, which will in turn result in individual and collective prosperity.

What are necessary etiquettes for a business organisation to practise?
Any business organisation must:

- Take sustainable and social responsibility
- Be ethical and look after the welfare of employees
- Take actions that factor in the long-term benefit of the organisation

On the issue of corporate governance, what is your advice to the management?
People have lost faith and trust in the corporate sector after all the recent scams. Business runs on trust and that trust needs to be reinstated. A few things worth considering:
- Is your corporation involved in social service projects or

are you active only in business?

- You cannot forget the welfare of your employees. You cannot think only along the lines of giving them a monetary raise. Such motivation runs dry very soon. You have to inculcate a sense of belongingness and caring.

- Another thing that the management needs to keep in check is the element of greed. Greed kills the customer first, and then the business. You do need to be ambitious but not at the cost of ethics or human values. Competition is fine, but within the limits of ethical practises, and there should be clear guidelines for both workers and management to adhere to.

- Top management should be concerned with the 'what' (goals of the organisation), middle management should be concerned with the 'how' and 'when' (process of achieving the goals) and lower management should be concerned with ensuring the quality of the output. If each of these is in place, you will find that there is such integrity in the whole system. So, if the lowest rung of management take responsibility for the quality, what is there to worry about? But in that case, have you inculcated that level of commitment in that stratum of workers? If not, what can you do to achieve it? This is where we come in. We have experimented, by giving people these Art of Living courses and workshops on belongingness.

- We sometimes ask the worker, "Suppose you are the owner of this company, what would you do?" See yourself in a different perspective. This is an ancient, Vedantic way of thinking, which asks you to put yourself in others' shoes and then see how your awareness expands, how your sense of belongingness grows. Imagine yourself in another's situation, ask yourself, "If I were in that person's place, what I would do?" This is the kind of education we really need. When people see life from different perspectives, there is such an expansion in consciousness. And from time to time, getting together, sitting and meditating for a few minutes, will help to create the requisite positive attitude and team spirit.

- Today, we need to develop a global outlook. We should imbibe teamwork from the Japanese, precision from the Germans, marketing skills from the Americans and spiritual values from the Indians.

Guruji, you have talked about love and of course, love is wonderful — you said God is love. But being a lawyer, I know of a famous saying, that when love goes out of the door, lawyers enter through the window. If there had been any love in the marriage, no lawyer would be needed. Isn't it a bit unrealistic that everybody is expected to be loving all the time?

You have no escape from love. Really. You are made up of a substance called love. If you are angry, it is because of love. You love perfection, and so you are angry at imperfection. When love gets distorted, it becomes anger. When love gets fermented, it becomes hatred. Your love for objects becomes greed. You love someone so much, that it becomes possessiveness and then it creates jealousy. Perhaps the world would have been a better place without love because of all these negative imperfections. In fact, love is the mother of all lawyers. If there were no love, then law as a profession would not survive. All negative emotions are nothing but distortions of love. I do not think love is an emotion that would make you say, "Oh my dear, I can't live without you, I want you to sit next to me all the time." Love is really what we are, it is our very existence, our whole life. But the way we express it, what we do out of love is a different thing. That needs wisdom.

I will give you an example. We run schools in the rural areas. Though everything is given free of cost to children, sometimes the attendance is very low. We have 100 children enrolled in a particular school in a tribal village and the attendance there is only 60%. So then we employ *Ayahs* (helpers), who personally go and fetch the children from every home. And sometimes, because these children are the first generation literates (in their families), if they start crying, the mothers do not want them to go to school. They tell them, "Do not worry. You take care of the goats and sheep and chickens, you don't have to go to school." So we have to do a lot to convince them and persuade them to send the children. And we offer a lot of incentives for the children to come to school. We give them toys and sweets every day. Of course, once they are a part of the system, they follow the rules. Now you understand, this is why I say, the love of those who are ignorant is harmful and even the anger of the wise is good.

Guruji, you have not spoken about religion. What is your take on it? There are so many religions practised in the world. Does religion come in the way of love? Does it come in the way of being a global human being?

No, not at all. I often say religion is like the banana skin, and spirituality is the banana, the substance. You see, there are three aspects to religion. First, its practises, second, its symbols, third, its values. Values are common to all the religions whereas practises and symbols vary from one religion to another; even within a religion, they vary from one sect to another. Diversity is in our very nature, so we accept the diversity all around us. And it is only healthy to view all religions with a sense of belongingness and inclusiveness, rather than alienate one from the other.

A child who is taught only about his own religion and its practises, who is not exposed to other forms of knowledge, will feel commitment only towards his own faith. But when his awareness expands, he will think, "I thought I would go to heaven after some time, but I now feel heaven is right here, when we love and serve everybody around us equally." It is this understanding we need to strive towards. If every child on this planet learns a little bit about all the different religions of the world, that will be the end of terrorism; children would grow up to be really strong and loving individuals. It is because we have not educated our children enough, because we restrict their learning, that they think it is wrong to practise other religions. We need to break these narrow boundaries and bring in a globalised wisdom.

Some of us run businesses. I run my own business and there are problems of various types I encounter every day. They could be related to production, to finance, to personnel — all sorts of problems. How do we solve them?

During the course of a day at work, we may get upset, at times we may have a frown on our faces or talk to people too roughly. At the end of the day, some problems are solved, some are not. Those that remain unresolved, we try to come back to them at a later date and try afresh to find a solution. Now I want to know from you Guruji, if we were to show compassion and love, if we were to smile as often as possible, how is that going to help really? I mean, if I call in my staff and try to explain these things, I don't know how any problem to do with a production-related issue will get resolved by love or compassion. I mean, these problems are addressed on a daily basis in the usual way we know, and at the end of the day, we are OK I guess, but maybe we are not OK from your perspective.

Ok, I got your point. And yes, your team knows how to solve problems, using their expertise and experience. Tell me, what type of boss you would prefer, someone who always has a frown on his face, who puts pressure on you? If someone above you were like that all the time, you would either get frustrated or soon get used to his behaviour and stop caring about your own work, and your own commitment would flag. Anger needs to be shown, sometimes it becomes essential, I agree. I am not saying that as a leader, you should keep smiling in all situations. But you should use anger sparingly. Sometimes just a little expression of anger on your face gets a lot of work done much faster. But if you are angry every day, all the time, your anger actually loses its importance and efficiency. So, you would rather make people feel comfortable around you, and inspire them by smiling with them and being with them, understanding their point of view, creating a sense of belongingness in them, rather than run the business operating on fear psychosis, where people do as you say, mainly because they are afraid of you. Fear and anger should be used as an emergency brake, in a limited fashion.

Guruji, how does one deal with corruption in society? Every day you go to the office as CEO or managing director of the company and you face a tremendous number of demands which are not fulfilled. This is a threat to your own business. It is happening to every one of us and we are not able to do very much about it. I do not say it is good or bad, but I do not know how to deal with it.

This is where meditation helps. When you are faced with tremendous pressure, unending deadlines, you do not need to drop dead, you only need to take a few minutes to relax and meditate. You will see then that the right, intuitive thoughts come at the right time and you feel such a confidence growing within you. Instead of seeing something as a problem, you begin to think of it as a challenge and find yourself enthusiastically solving it. Keeping your enthusiasm alive will really help you when you are under tremendous pressure.

Corruption in society. Yes, that is a big problem indeed. For that, we need to bring about a spiritual awareness in the society we live in. Do you know about the Kumbha Mela that happened in Allahabad three years ago? 30 million people were there and not a single crime occured. Can you imagine that? Everybody lived in tents, nobody lost anything, there was no theft, no corruption. How could that be? I wish the whole country could function like the Kumbha Mela. Where there is such a strong sense of togetherness and security, where if I need something, I know that there is going to be someone who will help me, who will be there for me. That is the mantra that will work against corruption. Again I tell you, the lack of belongingness is the cause of corruption. And we all need to fight it together. Have you heard about Anna Hazare? A single man backed by the force of simple villagers — many of them uneducated — they successfully fought corruption. They dismissed 450 officers who were corrupt. Action and initiative that comes from our volunteers in society, taking a step in the right direction, will definitely yield a positive result. It will not work tomorrow morning, but we have to work towards that goal.

I agree with you completely Guruji, it is evolution which we need to go through, as a society, but right now I am working hard to make sure my company survives. I am asked to pay money for various reasons, and I am told that if I do not, I will not get what I rightfully must have. How do I deal with all the commitment I have to my ethical values in such a scenario?

You have to weigh your choices. What is most important to you, to the long term goals of your company? You have to take into account individual circumstances. And with skill and discrimination you have to handle tricky situations that come your way.

Recent work in neuro-theology has suggested that the idea of communion with God is nothing but the sense of losing your orientation, that if you lose your orientation in time and space, you feel that you are a part of the universe. Is this true?

Someone who is ignorant would call it 'losing'. I would see it the other way — it is a sense of 'gaining'. Your orientation with the vast existence beyond you is what will help you find yourself.

In that context, how will you define God?

It is difficult to define that which cannot be defined. Yet, people think God is somebody sitting somewhere in heaven, that He is going to come and redeem you or that He is waiting to punish you if you make a mistake. This concept of God is what falls apart. When you meditate, when you are truly awake, it is not God sitting somewhere but God as the basis for existence itself, God as a fundamental part of your existence that will manifest to you. What is the difference between being asleep and awake? You are as alive when you are sleeping, as you are when you are awake, isn't it? You are breathing, your heart is functioning, your lungs are functioning, and so are all your other organs doing their job while you are sleeping. So, do you know what changes when you are awake? There is a shift. You do not know that you are sleeping when you are asleep. But when you wake up, you know you are awake. If you can establish this fundamental difference, you will be able to answer the questions, "What is?" and "Who am I?" I would say, if science tells us about what things are, spirituality tells us about who we are, and the two are really not at loggerheads at all.

I listened to the way you described the ABCD of governance, and I thought of another way of expanding the same — A for arrogance, B for bragging, C for conceit and D for deceit — because I feel these are the things that are actually hindering the ABCD you explained. Also, the e-governance we talk about these days has become ego-governance. So many people in the corporate sector think that spirituality is against economic prosperity. Could you kindly again throw some light on how the two are really not different? Thank you.

OK, let us see what spirituality can bring to us, apart from all the ABCDs. Spirituality brings with it enthusiasm. Now is enthusiasm against prosperity? No. Spirituality adds more time to your life because it gives you so much energy. If you meditate, if you follow spiritual practises, you gain so much more time in your life. You do not have to sleep for eight hours, four to five hours of sound sleep is good enough for you and it keeps you energised. So, this gives you time, enthusiasm, creativity, and endless energy. All these you require for prosperity.

To be creative, your mind has to be alert and in the present moment. Do you know why so many people in the R&D departments are lethargic? Because they are so tired. They have writers' blocks, thinking blocks, their minds are clogged, because they never give it the right kind of service! We take our cars to service, but never think of doing the same for our minds! So the mind is not energised. But spirituality energises you and brings you the intuition that is needed for business.

Guruji, I was wondering if you would share some personal thoughts with us. First, what is your own mission in life, and second, what is the source of your own motivation and energy?
Oh, I thought I have been talking personally all this time! What was my motivation to start this course? It was just like a poem. A poet writes a poem spontaneously. He does not know how. It just comes naturally to him. The same thing happened with these programmes. I am simply sharing what I have, what I know, with everyone. And what I would like to see is a smile on everybody's face, everyone becoming like a child again — simple, innocent and with a natural sense of belongingness. I would like to see a little children's world again.

Those striking terror in the world today — are they aware of the ABC you spoke about? They feel they belong to their particular religion or group, they are committed to the acts they undertake, yet their actions cause such mass destruction. What is going wrong there?

An expanded awareness and belongingness is required. See, even a corrupt person is committed to his family, to taking care of his loved ones. But we need to build a broad vision for life and a commitment to basic human values around us. 'Broaden your vision and deepen your roots' — this should be a slogan for our youth to work on today.

Our shastras say: "Ayamnijahparoveti gananaalaghuchetasaam udaaracharitaamtu vasudhaiva kutumbakam," *meaning, "The distinction of 'This is yours, this is mine' is for narrow-minded people. For a truly liberated person, the whole world is one family." That is a wonderful goal, no doubt. The trouble is that instead of having* vasudhaiva kutumbakam *(the world is one family), there is so much fight in that* kutumba *(family) itself. So, are we not on some unrealistic trip here?*

There may be so many obstacles, big and small, that you face, but do not drop your highest goals or your vision in life. For if your vision is big enough, you will be able to pull through any situation. I do not say that life will full of rose petals everywhere, that everything will be smooth. But we can overcome all manner of hurdles when we have a bigger goal, bigger vision. You do not stop because there is a problem in any one place. You need to continue with the same zeal that you started out with.

I want to quote a small Urdu couplet, then I will translate it.
"Yun to sadiyon se hai insaan ka wajood, aankh aaj bhi tarasti hai insaan ke liye..."
meaning,
"People have been in existence for centuries, but I have yet to find a good person." There is a dearth of good people in society. India is a country of saints, yet character erosion has been rampant in this country. Would you not blame religion for it? There are countries that give far less importance to religion and yet they produce good

people. Ours has become a country with too much of religion and too many bad people.

Why do not you see a good person? Close your eyes and start looking within, wherever you are.

Man meettha to jag meettha...

When you feel good about yourself, you will see good everywhere. I would say that about even those who commit crime, if you really get to know them, they are good people, but it's just that nobody taught them how to handle their emotions. So those we brand as criminals are not really evil, but in a weak moment of emotional upheaval, they impulsively did what they did. Because they did not know how to handle their minds at that moment. You should go and meet people in Tihar jail and really sit down and talk to them, you will understand what I am saying.

Yahaan to har aankh mein insaan kyon, khuda nazar aate hain. (In every eye I look into here, I behold not humans, but the Divine Itself.)

Hum khud ko ek baar dekh lein, phir humein khuda hi khuda nazar aayenge. (If we perceive ourselves just once, we will see nothing but God everywhere.)

Jahaan dekhoon jidhar, tu hi tu hai. (Wherever I see, I find You, and You alone.)

Do not think of people as bad human beings. I am yet to meet one bad person. If someone seems bad, he is driven by his circumstances, by a lack of understanding. I have just returned from Kashmir. Yesterday, I met people who have been terrorists. I asked four of them, "What do you want to do?" They said, "Guruji, *aap bataayiye hum kya karein.* Till yesterday, we carried guns. Today, you tell us what we should do."

So what did you tell them?

I just smiled at them. They had already sensed the affection I felt for them by then, and they said, "We have never experienced so much love in our life. You lit the lamp in us today, you have to hold us to this. You should come back here more often. That is our only request."

When we look at people with loving eyes, there is love even in that simple gesture. And that love reflects back at us. If you think, everybody around you is a cheat, everybody is a *Vishwasghaati* (a betrayer), then you get trapped in that illusion of evil yourself. What do you say?

How do we tap emotional intelligence in people at the work place?
Emotional intelligence surfaces when emotions become refined and refined emotions can only result from a stress-free life.

How does The Art of Living help an individual to manage conflicting expectations and demands within the family and in organisations?
Demand, capability and performance, these are the three factors that you need to look at. If the performance is good, demand will naturally increase, and then you need to direct your attention to that source of power, of spiritual energy that you have within you.

Could you give us some tips on stress management?
These mantras I have already given to you in the very beginning. CCC — cosmology, commitment, compassion. If you cultivate compassion, you will have no stress. If you have commitment, you do not mind the stress, and if you have a broad vision, rest assured that stress does not come anywhere near you.

As lawyers, we deal with conflicts all the time. I am wondering if you have any comments, specifically for us. In a negotiation, we try to get to a win-win situation, but at the litigation stage, both sides lose. What are the key principles that you think we need to follow?

I think you just need to be intuitive and spontaneous. There is no ready-made solution or formula to resolve conflicts. When you are in that moment, be spontaneous, be intuitive and retain a sense of humour. That will ease your mind first, and then it will ease the situation too.

Can you tell us about time management, because that is a challenge that all of us lawyers face. We cannot really manage time as well as we would like to.

First, we should know the reverse — that time is managing us in some way. The lazy have all the time, the un-intelligent have no time and the intelligent will make time. It is the same 24 hours in a day, whether for a clerk in a bank or for the Prime Minister. The difference lies in the responsibilities they both take. We should know that it is the restlessness in us that makes us feel that we are short of time. If you are relaxed and if you are intuitive, then you will find that you have all the time, that you can make time, you can do it. Just that bit of confidence in your mind will let you find time when you need it most. Of course, a few minutes of meditation will always help. And it can also reduce your sleep requirement as I said earlier. Four hours of good sleep with half an hour of meditation in the morning and in the evening can help you.

Can you say something about how we can improve when we are in the habit of being impulsive?

If you are impulsive, you put people off very fast. If you have control over yourself, you won't take hasty decisions. You will listen to both sides of the story and take a decision only when the mind is quite calm and rational.

One of the techniques we teach in the APEX course is that whenever you have an important decision to make, you should wait for 15 seconds — take a couple of deep breaths during that time. Then, you will see that most of the time, your decision will not be wrong.

What is the difference between a leader and a follower?
A true leader creates more leaders. He does not simply create followers. A chain of leaders are being created in the Art of Living programme.

A leader is one who takes total responsibility. A follower is one who thinks someone else should do the job and gives the responsibility to someone else. In our organisation this is not how it works. Everyone is taught how to take responsibility and is capable of doing it.

Isn't a lack of leadership the problem in our country today?
Yes it is. There is an institute for every discipline, but I don't think any such thing exists in the field of politics! We should have an institute for politics too, where training should be given on how to conduct, manage and care for the country. A broad vision has to be taught to the people. Probably, if we had such institutions, mikes and chairs wouldn't be broken so regularly in the parliamentary assembly!

Even if I follow all this **sattvik gyan** *in thought, mind and actions, I may still be suffering because of my past karmas. Is it because we have a political system today in the country based on our past karmas, that we are all suffering thus?*
It is more than just a few bad guys doing bad things. The lethargy or unwillingness to act on the part of the good people has caused this present scenario. It is due to their silence and inaction that the situation has come to what it is. So, now people simply have to wake up. We have slept a little too long. 40 years ago, politicians had some respect; when they went somewhere, they commanded

some respect quite naturally. Today, people avoid them! That whole profession, that whole stratum of people has lost its charm and glory. I believe right after Independence, people stepped into the field of politics as a *seva,* a service. Today, politicians are businessmen. They are becoming politicians so that they can make money, not because they can serve the country. It is the wrong attitude in the wrong place.

Guruji, you mentioned that creativity can only come from a calm and composed mind. With the way we work nowadays and the way we are living nowadays, what do you advise as dinacharya, *that will help us to have a calm mind?*
It would help immensely if you learn some breathing exercises, such as *pranayam or Sudarshan Kriya... Sudarshan Kriya* is very good. You do it for 10 minutes and it keeps your energy levels high through the day. In the afternoon or evening, for a few minutes you could sit and relax, do meditation. To begin with, you can try some guided meditation using audio CDs, later on you can do it on your own, without any other external help. Then you must spend some time listening to music. So that the right brain and left brain are balanced. If a right brain activity, like music, is absent from your day, and if you are using only your left brain constantly, then you grow more tired, agitated, restless. Once in a while, you should take time out to indulge in activities outside your routine, for example, go to a garden or do some gardening. If you do a few simple things like these, you will find that it relaxes you deeply.

Guruji, how does spirituality bring about accountability?
Accountability is essential, particularly where there is no honesty. If you are not honest to yourself, then you have to be accountable to somebody else. But when you are in touch with your inner self, when you are spiritually inclined, you cannot be dishonest to yourself. Just the way no man can be corrupt with his own family.

Now extend that a little further. And you will find no one can be corrupt with his own team or community, and seen from that angle, you will find that you feel a sense of belongingness with everybody, so you cannot be corrupt at all. Do you understand what I am saying?

Yes, this is a very glossy picture I am presenting, and you may wonder whether it is possible to really achieve it. You are probably thinking, it all sounds so great, but is it practical? When I began offering these Art of Living courses and meditation programmes, many people had the same doubt. "What is Guruji saying? So many people are going to participate in these programmes. It is not possible to achieve such a lofty goal." They said it was just a dream. I tell you, every innovation, every creative development on this planet has happened thanks to an impossible dream. Hold on to an impossible dream and you will see that it will come true.

I am on a spiritual path and I also look for material success, and many times I face very conflicting situations. For example, I may be in a business that makes products which are harmful to consumers, such as pesticides. Or it could be something more harmful, such as cigarettes. How do I integrate something like that with my spiritual self? If I stay on the spiritual path, I feel that I am at a material loss. How do I manage to gain both materially and spiritually?

Four things are needed in life. And balancing these four things makes life comfortable.

First is *mukti* (freedom). Do you feel free? Or do you feel totally bound? The degree of your freedom determines the degree of your happiness.

Second is *bhakti* (love). What is it that you love? Do you love your values? Do you love your commitments? Do you love the society you are a part of? And how much do you love these things?

The third is *yukti* (skill). It is not good enough to say, "I am good as I am," or "I am very spiritual." You need to be intelligent and skillful at all times.

The fourth is *shakti* (strength).

To be successful in life, you need the first two things, freedom and love. And to be successful in this world, you need strength and skill. The right combination of all these four things can make you successful and fulfilled.

Coming to the point you made that some businesses may be harmful, the same question has been addressed in the Mahabharata too. There was a butcher who used to sell meat. That was his profession. So the question was raised — "Is this a correct profession to pursue?" The answer that he received was — "You are part of a profession that has been around for many years. You are not attached to it personally. You do your work with neither any craving nor any aversion. When you are a part of your profession in a detached way, it is ok." But let me add that if you think it is harmful for people and if you have the strength and skill to change this aspect of your profession, you should not hesitate to do it.

Guruji, if spirituality is the right way for society to progress, then why has India not progressed much as compared to other countries like the US?

When you compare India with America, you have to keep in mind that America is a relatively young country. It's only 400 years old whereas India is 5,000 years old. If you read a description of what Brindavan once was and if you go to Brindavan today, you will be shocked. What it was like 5,000 years ago, with so many trees and such peace, and if you compare that with what it is like today — you will realise there is just no comparison! This is what I would say about comparing India and the US — our country has one third of the land America does, three times their population, we have 22 different languages, 600 hundred dialects, so many religions and ethnic groups, and a 1,000 years of slavery, and in spite of all these, India is still alive! It is a miracle, no less! And surely we are still progressing. Otherwise we would have gone to pieces, as former Yugoslavia did.

It is not our culture that is to blame for the poverty in the country. It is our lack of self esteem. Perhaps, it is an outcome of so many years of slavery. The youth today need to be infused with self esteem and national pride. When you tell somebody they are hopeless over and over, they really become hopeless. This is what has happened with India. Our biggest drawback is our habit of deprecating ourselves, blaming ourselves for everything wrong. This country is strong and rich and vibrant even today, because there is unity in diversity, and there is some spirituality in the environment, and these things are responsible for keeping things together, helping people still moving ahead.

Often it seems to us that the other side is much rosier. Sitting here in India, we think Europe is much better. We go to Europe and find that there are numerous problems they have. One child in every ten goes to a psychiatrist. In Washington DC alone, 33% of the youth have gone to prison at least once, and that is an unhealthy number, I think. Depression and crime rates are high in all developed countries.

My point is, we need to look at ourselves from a global perspective. We need to learn the best there is to learn from everybody around us in the world.

Learn team work from the Japanese — they are excellent at team work.

Learn precision from the Germans — anything they do, they do it in the best way possible, with such precision.

Learn negotiating and marketing from the Americans — they are very good at it.

And learn human values from Indians. When you meet someone in a village in India, you may find that man has just one meal for himself, but he will still share that meal with you. People in our villages may not have much, but they definitely have a smile on their face. They have compassion, they are full of friendliness.

Sometimes I ask my teachers to try out this exercise. I tell them to go to somewhere far away from the city. They go up to some villagers and tell them that they have lost everything and need some money to get back home. Do you know who helps them the most? Poor people. The person who has a jewelry shop does not give five rupees. But the man who sells vegetables on a handcart says, "Oh, you are robbed of all your money, I'll give you some." And he gives them 20 rupees. This is the experience our people have actually had!

Those who have very little themselves, have more to share with others. This is amazing. We do this exercise to get a taste of how people respond, to see what values they practise. And we find that love, compassion, empathy, all these human values are very much alive. All is not dead.

How can one find job satisfaction, Guruji?
This term 'job satisfaction' does not exist, or it exists only in dictionaries. Satisfaction comes to you when you do some service. Your job is a duty you are fulfilling, it is not at all the same as service.

How can one make one's job interesting? Your very willingness to make a task interesting makes a difference. There is no readymade formula here. You have to innovate. You take a conscious decision — today I am not going to get bored. Anything that I do, I am going to thoroughly enjoy. Take this one determined decision. Try doing this, take it up as a challenge, and you will find that your job is not the same.

In today's world, it seems that selling spiritual knowledge generates most wealth. So in the corporate world too, should we

start selling only spiritual knowledge, so that we gain the highest wealth and the most amount of happiness?

First of all, if you think your happiness is measured only in wealth, you are mistaken. There was a study conducted recently. Do you know where the happiest people in the world live? Nigeria, followed by Bangladesh. India comes in, I think, at the 5th or 6th place. It is not through wealth that you achieve happiness, forget about it. You may have enough wealth but you may not be able to eat all the food you can buy. You may have diabetes or high cholesterol. You will have to eat food without *ghee* (clarified butter) and *sookha roti* (dry bread). You may have a comfortable bed, but you may not be able to sleep — you may suffer from insomnia. Half the health we have is spent to gain wealth, and then we spend half of that wealth to recover the health we have lost! I do not think this is an intelligent way to live.

The other thing that you asked about, that spirituality seems to be flourishing — Tirupati earns a revenue of 1000 crores, Sabarimala too earns in crores. So should we leave the corporate world and take up religion as a business?

If you think of spirituality as a business, neither business nor spirituality will really work. When spirituality is adopted as a service, whatever is needed to carry out the projects you include in your service to society, all those requirements take care of themselves. When you live spiritually, you take little, you give more. In business, you take more and give less. And this is the correct formula. If you do business the way you practise spirituality, you will have to shut down very soon! If you buy raw material worth 100 rupees and sell it somewhere for 80 rupees, how long can you do it? You will always need to make a profit by buying something at 80 rupees and selling it at 100 rupees. You give less and take more. That's the way business works. But when exercising spirituality, you take only a little and try to give back more, so that you feel a sense of connection and communication, a sense of having done something. Both these ways of being are based on different mathematics, but both are needed for human life.

Guruji, is the purpose of this seminar to integrate both spiritual and material happiness?

First of all, they are not at loggerheads with each other. Lakshmi (Goddess of wealth) and Narayana (Protector of the world) are not fighting. They are not filing for divorce!

Take some time off and dedicate yourself to social service. Spiritual life involves a taking little time off to yourself, to ponder about your own life — "Who am I? What am I doing? What is the purpose of my life? Am I going to go on living like this — eating, drinking, sleeping, watching television, until one day I kick the bucket?" You do not even know when you are going to die. All the cheque books and all the bank balances are left behind for somebody else to handle, for your children, who then fight over all that was yours. Do you know about 70% of court cases are about inheritance issues. You will be surprised to hear this. So you see, you need to reflect over what your life is really about.

Secondly, do whatever *seva* or service you can, without expecting anything in return. It gives you immense satisfaction. There are two types of joy. One is the joy in getting something — this is like the joy a child feels. A child wants to grab everything in sight. Take a child to a toy shop. If he has his way, he would bring the entire shop home. This is a childish joy. Then, there is a mature kind of joy, the joy of a grandmother at home. The grandmother does not make 10 types of dishes and eat them all herself. Yes, she makes many types of food, but her joy is in feeding children, isn't it? How many ladies here will agree with me? When the woman is alone at home, she may not even cook. She prepares so many types of food only when there are others whom she can feed. So we need to grow from the joy of getting to the joy of giving. That is what makes your life very rich and satisfied.

Guruji, what can I personally gain from spirituality?

Spirituality is not about "what can I get" but "what I can give." Spirituality brings about this shift in you, makes you go from "how I can use others" to "how useful I can be to others." Imagine if everyone thought in terms of "how can I make use of the other person," would the world be a good place? Do you know how wealth is created? By doing something useful. You publish a paper which is read by everybody, you become wealthy. You prepare food which is needed by everybody, and then you become wealthy. Everybody needs cell phones. You create the desired product that meets the needs of the people, then you become wealthy, isn't it? So instead of saying, "what will I get from spirituality at the end of the day," you can think of it this way — spirituality is the factor that brings meaning to your life, that makes you blossom, that makes you happy, that makes you share and care.

We see such a lot of migration from India to other countries. When people go abroad, their productivity improves. For some people, in their own families they were labelled "good for nothing." They went abroad and then they showed tremendous improvement in productivity! Probably none of them went through any of these exercises or programmes. The funny thing is that while all this is available in our great nation, the moment they fly out, as soon as they take a six hour flight out of this country, they all become more productive. Is it something in the environment, is it to do with the individual? The same person within a few weeks is now a changed man!

It's a question of survival outside. Here, somehow you can get by, but when you go out of your comfort zone to a new place, your survival is at stake. You have to compete with different people in different situations, and many Indian businessmen who go out also face the fear of racial discrimination. There are many other such uncertainties which push them to work harder. And when they come to me, they ask, "Guruji, we are so tired of this life, can we go back to India?" And I tell them, "No, stay here. Continue to work hard."

How do we deal with people who create a negative atmosphere in the office?
You know, there will always be some people who are negative, who pull others down. You educate them and then you ignore them. These irritants are present just to challenge you, to help bring out the people skills in you. To teach you how to manage people in a tough situation. Anyone can work in a comfortable, familiar situation but it needs extra intelligence and wisdom to work with people with negative and obstructing mentalities. You develop patience when you meditate every day, and your positive vibrations will change the whole atmosphere.

Today we find many people who come into the industry not by choice; maybe they wanted to do something else but ended up where they are instead. Guruji, when you talk about motivation and inspiration, how do we deal with such people in the organisation?
When a person is mentally stressed, you cannot expect much from him. Merely giving him a paycheck is not enough. As an employer, you have to know whether his mental health is ok, whether he has a reason to smile, whether he is enthusiastic in doing his job. And that is where the Art of Living programme comes in. Wherever we conduct our sessions, we relieve people of their stress, making them physically fit and healthy. It is like teaching personal hygiene — only this is mental hygiene we are talking about. If you have not taught a person how to handle his negative emotions, how to live in the present moment, how to have presence of mind, creativity and a sense of belongingness at the work place, how can you expect better work culture? There is a difference between a businessman and a worker. A businessman feels a sense of ownership, he sees

it as his own company, whereas a worker does not bother about things like that. And this is what is called karma yoga. We can play any of our roles in life either in the karma yoga fashion or in the akarma yogi fashion. You can be a karma yogi school teacher or an akarma yogi school teacher. The former is one who takes interest in the child, gives him one or two special sessions, sees that the child's problems are eliminated and ensures that he moves ahead. The latter type of teacher thinks, "Why do I care? Let his parents take care of him." The same is true of a karma yogi patient and an akarma yogi patient. The former is one who goes by the advice of the doctor. The latter simply takes the medicine, puts it under the pillow and sleeps. He does not take the medicine at all and then blames the doctor when there's no improvement. So we need to bring about a change in this attitude and that can happen only through meditation.

How do we promote creativity at the workplace?
When there is tremendous pressure on a person, it does not allow him to be creative. Here spirituality and yoga come to your rescue. When there are too many deadlines to meet, take a few minutes to calm down, relax, look deep within yourself and you will find you are able to come up with many ideas, brilliant ideas. Now the dilemma is whether creativity is nurtured in the midst of chaos or whether it is to be found when in a calm and collected state of mind. I would say it is to be found somewhere in between. If chaotic conditions alone encouraged creativity, Iraq would have been the most creative zone in the past few years; there is enough chaos there. Lebanon too, for the last 20 years, has been in chaos. And so is the situation in some other parts of the world. They all would have been the most creative countries today, but we do not see that happening. So, it is not really true that chaos is the best breeding ground for creativity. On the other hand, if just being very calm and quiet is the source of creativity, we find that even that is not necessarily true.

Greenland is very calm, Iceland is even calmer. In Finland and many other Scandinavian countries, people have everything; all their basic needs are met. But we do not see that great creativity has emerged from those corners of the world either. So you see, it is not something to be found in the geographical location, we need to look within. It has nothing to do with what is outside you; it has something to do with what is within you. You are a part of God and God is creative, and so you are creative. Get in touch with that Divinity deep within you. That brings forth all the creativity and values we need, and realising and implementing this can be encapsulated in one word — spirituality.

In corporate life, we are faced with situations where we have to fire some people, and this leaves us with a sense of guilt, leaves us wondering whether we are doing the right thing, especially when we know that these guys will probably be without a job for some time. How does one deal with this guilt?
You should not mix business and charity. If you run your business like a charity, you are going to be finished. And so also, a charitable undertaking should not be run as a business. These are two separate things.

If you see, in most NGOs, the overheads are enormous, almost 50-60% of the expenses. As I said in the Art of Living programme, your overheads should not cross 3-5%. All the revenues, stationery and everything else you spend on, should fall within that amount set aside.

This is why I say that you do business using your head and you do charity using your heart.

In personal life, we follow some principles, but in corporate life, sometimes we need to compromise on ethics for the benefit of the company. How do we find a balance?
You just said it yourself — balance it! Yes, it takes a lot of courage

and commitment to stand up to your values in all situations. If you can do it, that is the best way out. But if you cannot do it, for the sake of the company, you can make small concessions, but only as much as salt in the food. The *shastras* also say there is a limit to how many lies a businessman is allowed.

Often, the needs of the organisation are in conflict with the needs of the individual, which are the happiness and success of his family, who need him. The constant struggle is that the organisation's definition of success is always contrary to the individual's definition of happiness, celebration, relaxation. How can we find the way out of this?

Conflict is not contained in any situation, conflict exists only in our mind. If you find yourself in a conflicting situation, where there is a problem and you are unable to smile, you need to find a way to fix it yourself. When I was in Iraq, I spent some time sitting and talking with the people there. They were all having a great time! They were laughing, cracking jokes and playing. You may wonder — a country which is on fire, where lakhs of women have been widowed and so many children orphaned, where people are battling enormous problems, including no electricity, no water, no sanitation, and radiation in the food, but despite all these problems, their people are happy, sitting and talking, laughing and planning their vacation. I was happy to see how cheerful they were. If they turned miserable, what good would that be?

What I am saying is that if too many demands are put on you, for the success of the company, you should not lose heart. Come what may, keep your spirits high.

I think that bringing spirituality to business, as you have propagated for many years now, has been very beneficial to the country, to the world, but now I think the reverse seems to be happening — we seem to be bringing business into spirituality.

How do we avoid that?

In our country, we think that business is not a good thing to do. People say, "Oh he's made a business out of it," as though business is a crime. Our thinking is inhibited by this kind of attitude.

See, charity cannot be done using an empty bowl. Any spiritual organisation is expected to do some amount of charity, because charity is a part of spirituality. So that means the organisation must have some way of earning money. The other way to go about it is to beg. But begging on one hand, while doing charity on the other, is no good. So it is wise for spiritual organisations to charge a little for the services they provide. I do not think there is anything wrong in that, it is even a part of our tradition. No knowledge should be given without *dakshina*. When you charge a fee for learning, people take it seriously. They attach value to it. You teach someone the same *pranayama* for free, they come along and halfway through the class, they will get up and go out to pick up their aunt from the railway station! But if they pay 500 rupees… they will stay put and take the class seriously! This has been our own experience. In the beginning, in India, I would teach all these courses free of charge, or on the basis of some donation. And of course, when Swamis or Gurus teach, people come and sit attentively, but when they find other teachers conducting the session, it becomes a problem. There was a lack of commitment that we experienced.

You will have seen, if a physics professor gives free tuition, barely 10 students attend his class. But when the same physics professor starts charging 1,000 rupees for tuition, you will find 100 students queuing up! Because they think, "We paid him 1,000 rupees, we have to learn." They will not miss a single class. Our experience has been the same. In foreign countries, when we taught our courses for free in the beginning, they were all suspicious and apprehensive. Then we said, "We are going to teach you breathing techniques, yoga and meditation, and this is the fee — 100 dollars." That instantly put people's minds at rest! So I would say that it is better to find ways to make people understand. Art of Living has always maintained self reliance in every area and we do charity only as much as we can do.

We are buffeted today by two opposing theories. One is the theory of karma which would have us believe that a lot of what is happening is pre-ordained, and there is a completely different theory at the other end of the spectrum, which says that the universe is a machine, and if you have the right intention, you can do exactly what you believe in. Now how do both of these connect together, and how does it relate to what we need to do by way of action in corporate life, particularly in the context of spirituality? The concept of karma is one of the most brilliant principles in the world which has kept people going. It prevents people from going insane. It has helped us a great deal, in balancing our mental health. When you see it as your karma, you do not hold a grudge against others. We are more peaceful within ourselves then, because we accept.

Then, there is something called *sankalpa*. All the *pujas* and *homas*, all the ceremonies that we practise, have a component called *sankalpa*. There is a difference between a desire, a wish and *sankalpa* or intention. Desire is something which clogs your mind in feverishness. Suppose you want to go to Pune for a personal reason tomorrow. Then all of today, and the whole way to Pune, you keep obsessing over your visit, so much so that you go insane before you reach Pune!

But with one singular intention — that of going to Pune — you stop at Lonavala and couple of other places on the way maybe, and then you reach Pune. All the way there, you may be talking or doing something else, but without any feverishness. This is how intention works differently from desire.

Sankalpa is what leads to *siddhi* (perfection). It is an ancient concept. The past is karma, in the present, you must do your karma, and the future is the *agami* karma — whatever you will do in the future is based on your sankalpa. There is no conflict within these principles. Accept the past, plan for the future and live in the present moment.

What would you say to people who are sceptical of meditation?
Actually, I would tell them that they are lagging behind in time. People were skeptical 30 years ago probably. Today the world over, people have recognised the importance of breathing, the importance of meditation. Even when you are in an aircraft, you have a channel — as in Lufthansa Airlines, you have a Channel 13, which tells you to breathe deeply and meditate. So you see, guided meditation has become a part of almost all progressive industry today. Have you seen that advertisement for Daimler Chrysler? Where a model is sitting in meditation and intoning, "Relax." Relaxation and meditation, this is the only way to get over depression, to get over lethargy and fatigue, and it has been proved over and over, that it can help maintain both the physical and the mental health of a person.

If you want to be healthy and creative, you cannot remain sceptical. Just the way, wherever you find you stand to gain from good dividends, wherever you see a good profit coming your way, you are not sceptical. People in business cannot afford to be doubtful on any front. Because if they are in doubt, then they are bound to lose, because they are not looking at the opportunity in the situation. I would advise people in the industry not to stick to the old paradigms. Wake up and move with the times. In our APEX program (Achieving Personal Excellence) we say, "Let out the steam, and get into the team." It is a course tailor-made for people in business and industry. It teaches many ways to see how a multinational or international company can cope with human resource problems and achieve personal excellence in their personnel departments.

When is authority required and what is the best motivation factor?
We need authority when there is no commitment within us. When you love something, you do it naturally. Sometimes I have to go and ask people working in our ashram to stop working so much and tell them to go sleep! Nobody tells them about what work they need to do but they have a high sense of commitment towards their work. And they work day and night to finish their tasks.

So the greatest motivating factor is our own commitment. When this is lacking, you have to look outside for something else to motivate you. Sometimes when there is too much love, it throws discipline off balance and there is chaos. But that of course, is sweet chaos.

There is a proverb which goes — Familiarity breeds contempt. This is only with reference to people who are not spiritual. If you have a spiritual component in you and have a broad vision, then the closer people come to you, the more they are amazed by you, and the more inspired they become. In this case, familiarity does not bring contempt but amazement, a feeling of "Ah!"

What should we do to take India forward today?
There are seven aspects in which India can really excel, provided we show efficient management.

1.   **Tourism** — India has the best tourism prospects in the world. We have the best beaches, snow-covered mountains and ancient monuments, like nowhere else in the world. People go to Egypt to see monuments that are just two and a half thousand years old, whereas the monuments in India are five to ten thousand years old. The temples in Tamil Nadu are a marvel but we don't realise it. We have abundant opportunities for tourism but we have never exploited them.

2.   **Ayurveda** — Today, Ayurveda is called the 21st century medicine; the medicine without side-effects. It is pure and helps in

treating all kinds of health issues. It is an established science but we are very slow in harnessing it in our own country. Panchakarma (an Ayurvedic treatment) which was practised in the remote villages of Kerala is only now gaining popularity after the West took to it. Panchkarma treatment in the West costs around $7000. That's when you come back to India and realise how wonderful this system of medicine we've always had is!

I know a couple from California who came and lived in India for four years. They took back many medicinal herbs and plants from Kerala and set up a culture farm for these plants in California. They claim that they can supply as many herbs and plants as required and that these are of the best quality! We have not even attempted, in our country, to develop such herbal resources that are already available here.

3. **Food** — India has so many varieties of cuisine in every state; whether it is *avial* from Kerala, sweets from Bengal, *pooran poli* from Maharashtra or *masala dosa* from Tamil Nadu. There are varieties of food that are tastier and healthier than pizzas. But we have not popularised them. When we conduct our courses abroad, many different Indian food items are offered and people just love it.

4. **Spirituality and Yoga** — Yoga is a 27 billion dollar industry in America alone! And most of it is owned by Americans. We have disowned our yoga and our spirituality. The well-known movie 'Matrix' is based on a scripture called Yoga Vashishta. It is a beautiful treatise describing the knowledge of yoga given to Sri Rama by Sage Vashishta. This book is published by New York University.

More than 100 universities abroad now have Vedic studies — Indology — but these courses are all taught by the local people. Hardly 2% of the professors teaching there are of Indian origin. This is because most of the Indians are not well-versed in such studies. We have such books on bookshelves all over our country and yet nobody cares to promote spirituality.

In our movies, we make a parody of sadhus and link them to fraudulent persons. Then this is the impression left in the minds of the people. I hold the Mumbai film community responsible for this. In neighbouring Sri Lanka and Thailand there is much respect for monks. In the Sri Lankan Prime Minister's office, there is respect for spirituality; so too, in Thailand. Pakistan has much respect for spirituality. When a plane takes off, they say, "Insha'Allah the plane will land in (such-and-such) place." And when their plane lands, they read from their holy book, the Qur'an.

It is not that all such things must be implemented. The point is that in all these places there is much respect for their religion and spiritual traditions. But it is not so across India. There are two states in India which claim not to respect spirituality or religion. They are Kerala and West Bengal. Kerala reports the highest suicide rate while West Bengal has the highest crime rate.

5. **Textiles** — The variety of garments available in India is really impressive. We do need to bring down the manufacturing costs, given our competition with China. But our textile industry is unique.

6. **Jewellery** — There is a lot of beautiful jewellery that is manufactured in India. We have amazing creativity and variety in terms of design and usage.

7. **IT or Information Technology** — We have already seen India's abundant potential in this sector in the last few years.

These are the seven areas that we need to promote more today, to make India stand out on the world map.

How can we implement the Art of Living model around the world? Many business schools, including Harvard, study our model. They come to India and they study how the Art of Living institution has spread its branches all over the world. So many people benefiting from it is a success story in itself. And we do have a business school. It is run in Goa.

I don't see a contradiction between what is studied in management colleges and what we teach. Interacting with people, observing how your own mind works and not taking impulsive decisions is the vital core of every business. Usually bookish knowledge is different from practical knowledge.

How can you practically assimilate and integrate by human interaction? The United Nations set up the United Nations Millennium Goal. They began a programme against poverty, 'Stand up, Speak Out'. In just two months, 7.5 million people around the world helped out. And the UN was extremely happy. Even countries like Panama and Costa Rica joined hands because there was an inspiration that came from within for such a cause.

Do you think we should honour nature more?
Absolutely! Caring for the environment is part of spirituality. That's why in India, before one cuts a tree, one has to take permission from the tree and promise it that five more of the same type will be planted in its place. Only then does one have the right to cut it. This is an ancient tradition you know. Mountains, rivers and trees were greatly respected in the past. This ancient custom has to be put into practise now. We should honour nature because we are inextricably a part of it.

A general comment made by many is that the younger generation are copying the West and trying to act differently. My personal feeling is that we lack national trends. Do you feel so, and can the situation be improved in any way?
Definitely! I want you to. Once, when I was in America, I gave everyone a creative project to do on their own. An elderly lady who was around 60 years old came up with the idea of making small handkerchiefs. She was very fragile but enthusiastic. She told us that

her handkerchiefs were the best in the world! She had 17 points to prove it too, for example. how big it should be when you pick it up, what type of hemming it should have around the edges when you hold it, what type of material it should be made of, and so on. Everybody was roaring with laughter when she went on about these details. Marketing skills should be learnt from the Americans!

We need to be proud of our national trends. We need to raise our self-confidence and self-esteem. One of the main reasons for unemployment in our country is this lack of self-esteem. How can the spirit of entrepreneurship flourish when people do not have optimum self-respect?! But at the same time, we need to learn many things from other countries too — team work from the Japanese, precision from the Germans, mannerisms from the British etc. And the world can learn human values from Indians. Similarly, Africans are by nature straight-forward, innocent and open-hearted.

The ability to learn useful things from all over the world needs to be combined with self-pride. Otherwise it will be a dry kind of self-pride, harboured under the illusion that one is great and doesn't want to take anything from anyone else. But this is not true. We do need to borrow from our neighbours in the world.

I once called about 500 youngsters from the villages, to meet with the Minister for Industry. I told them that I was with them and would support whatever project that they wanted to take up. The Director offered to support about 100 of any of their projects. The Government would finance them, and as an NGO we would give some capital, but they would have to choose a project and start working on it.

But they did not want to do anything! They had various excuses for not taking up each one of the suggested projects. All they wanted apparently was a Government job or a police job. The reason for this was their utter lack of self-confidence. We need to instill this in them. And that is the reason we have started the Youth Leadership Training Programme. It is proving to be quite successful but we still have a lot to do.

Guruji, when it is my mind in question, why should anyone else teach me how to control it?

Your legs will operate a car, no doubt, but you still have to learn to drive. The accelerator is in your car. The legs and hands are yours. So, why should someone else teach you to drive?

The IITs have the maximum rate of suicides in the country. It is not poor children but academically brilliant children who are committing suicide! This alarming fact appeared in one of our country's national magazines.

Emotional problems do exist in schools and colleges. Nobody teaches us how to handle our anger. And that is why I said, there is a connection between breath and your emotions. When you are angry, your breath moves in a particular rhythm. When you are upset, your breath moves in another rhythm. When you are jealous, your breath moves in a different rhythm as compared with when you are depressed. You need to learn about this; about how you can handle your emotions and mind through the rhythms of the breath. You need to keep an open mind.

The Swiss were leaders in the watch industry till the late 70's and the early 80's. They dominated the world market. Then their position declined. It seems a young boy from the US had come up with the idea for a digital clock. He had approached all the Swiss companies to sell his product. But they had brushed him off, telling him that he could not possibly teach them about watches, that they were the market leaders. The boy then sold the patent in Boston, America and within a year, 60% of the Swiss companies had to close down because of the revolutionary sweep of digital clocks and watches all over the world.

There are four things that need revival. They are trade, technology, truth and tradition. You need to constantly revive them and try to understand them. The more you know, the more you are baffled and feel that you don't really know much.

Knowledge should lead you to a position where you feel that you do not know much, that there is much more to learn. If knowledge makes you think that you know everything, then you have closed yourself. You have covered your face with a helmet. It is normal to cover your head with a helmet when you drive, but how can you see anything if you cover your entire face with it?

To be stress-free, you should sometimes do something silly, something simple. You need to come out of your little shell and feel free. You should not bother what the world will think. Let anyone think what they like. You should not let other people's opinions sway you. If there is love, enthusiasm and a sense of belongingness in you, then that is the real success in life.

While there is an awful lot of consumerism around us, there seems to be a significant amount of dissatisfaction. Have you had much opportunity to observe this from the perspective of human values? Could you offer a few insights please?
We see that material comfort alone does not really make a person comfortable. You may have a good bed to sleep on, but may be unable to sleep because of insomnia born of worry. You need to have a broad understanding about yourself and your priorities.

Clarity of the mind makes things much easier to deal with. Understanding basic emotions like love and interacting well with people around you is important. So is knowing what your ego, intellect or mind is saying. A few minutes of introspection and relaxation every day are vital.

It's very interesting to analyse how a normal 80 year old has spent his life. He has slept for 40 years. He has eaten food for 8-10 years. Another 8 years of his life have been spent in bathrooms and toilets. 15-20 years have been spent working and being stuck in traffic jams. And hardly 2-3 years being happy, smiling, loving people and sharing a sense of belongingness with everybody!

Introspection about your life and about how you can improve its quality can help you feel better about yourself. This intention itself will open many doors for a person.

How do you teach someone tolerance?

Tolerance itself is a negative word. You tolerate that which you don't like. I think we need to now move from tolerance to love. This is because when you are unfamiliar with something, you don't love it. You may even dislike it. You need to see it in a different light. You should learn about every culture and tradition in the world, and respect and honour all of them.

Harmony and diversity should be our education. The day we educate ourselves in this sense, we will have far fewer problems. We would not have to tolerate anything.

What is needed for good administration?

Patience and poise! If you are more intelligent than others around you, you cannot bear their foolishness. Administration requires the management of a variety of situations and it requires you to deal with a variety of people, and much patience is needed for that. The progress of the nation, of any society, depends, to a great extent, on the administration. It is a trying job because you might find yourself caught between the political establishment and the common people. And it is not necessary that the two always be in agreement.

Patience, endurance, a sharp intellect and presence of mind are needed to be able to deal with both parties in a just manner. A mindset that tends to be rooted in the present moment needs to be cultivated and nurtured.

Patience and sharpness of the mind can be developed by attending to the breath and engaging in meditation, and by practising some breathing exercises for a few minutes each day. It is believed that 20 minutes of meditation a day can give the same amount of rest, relaxation and energy that comes from 8 hours of sleep!

Breathing exercises improve perception, observation and expression, and all three of these abilities are vital. Of course, you must also smile more. That applies to all of us! Would you rather spend time with a person who smiles often or with someone who is stiff and surly? You will find that people who smile a lot are more compassionate and loving. Some people fear smiling. They think that if they smile, they will be taken advantage of! If you smile with all your heart, it can never be to your disadvantage. Smiling is also important for another reason — it helps improve your personality.

We all know that we need a well-developed, socially well-adjusted personality to overcome all the hurdles that life throws our way. Hurdles do not belong to nature. They arise when we are not in tune with our own nature. We create hurdles for ourselves. To get rid of them, we need to make a start by smiling and resolving to take positive action.

We should be able to feel one with the whole world. See the world as one family. It is important that we feel at home wherever we are, with whoever we are.

We should have the ability to learn good things from different people we meet, wherever we go. We are all the same breed after all, guised under the differences of race, colour and culture. The spirit of joy and enthusiasm should be strong within us, such that no one can take it away!

This process is the Art of Living. It does not matter what race we belong to, what religion we follow, or where we live. We must love all humanity.

We belong to the world and the world and all the beings in it belong to us!

How can we introduce spirituality in management schools?
Spirituality is not just one compartment of learning, it is to do with the

values we practise in life. Spirituality is doing everything with love and relaxation, with commitment and service and a broadminded attitude. It teaches us to imbibe the good from everyone, everywhere.

So what is the most important Management Mantra?

You know, mantras are always given secretly. As I am speaking, you need to pick up the mantra wherever it is. So tell me, what all did you pick up since the time I have been talking? Pearls always come in shells and have to be picked out of the shells. Got it?

Excerpt from H. H. Sri Sri Ravi Shankar's interaction with management students

Guruji, as we graduate now, what is the message that we should carry with us as managers?

Manage yourself well. Manage to keep the smile that you have on your face now and put that smile on others' faces. As managers, you need two important qualities. One is your ability to take criticism, and the second is, your ability to give constructive criticism. Are you good at both? Or is taking criticism your weak point? See that you do not have any such weak sides to you. Both receiving and giving criticism require courage. When someone is criticising you, they are doing a good thing because they are polishing you in some way. I would like our students to be so strong that they do not go off balance with a few words of criticism from someone. If it is valuable, you should be able to pay attention and work on it. If it is not valuable, just laugh at it. Laugh and let go.

In management, there is always a lot of competition. How do we deal with it?

You manage competition with confidence. You compete with yourself. Forget about others. When I first went to California to conduct a course — way back in 1986-87 — there were about 7 members. People told me, "Guruji, why did you come here? This place is so saturated with all kinds of New Age stuff. It is a waste of your time and money." Those days it was expensive to go and rent a place, to make all the necessary arrangements to hold a session like that. Our organisation was still in its nascent stages and everyone discouraged me. I just smiled. I did not say anything to them. I went to Montreal, in Canada. We used to have the biggest *satsangs* there. We conducted courses with around 100-200 people attending our programmes in Montreal. And when I came back the next year, again I said, "I will go to California, I will go to Los Angeles." And once more, the same thing happened. There were maybe 15 people in all in the classroom — and 5 of them had travelled with me. We had a studio to ourselves and there was some loud music being played next door. Now you know how Los Angeles music is! How do you chant "Soham, Soham" when there is a rock band playing at full volume right next to you?! It was sort of a disaster. So then again people told me, "Guruji, why do you come here? What you are trying to teach will not work in this place. This place is so saturated. Paramhamsa Yogananda has come and established his school here..." and they went on and on, telling me about all the various programmes in the area. And they would bring me these big newspapers, New Age magazines, which published on all sorts of themes — past life, future life and whatnot! I listened to them but it did not stop me, and I went visiting again. Now we have 7 centres in that area, right there in Los Angeles. And thousands of people come, they are all Art of Living people today. When I go, no hall is big enough to hold the crowd. Some of my best talks have been given there, about 7 such sessions. For instance, the Buddha - Manifestation of Silence talk. Have you heard that one — Buddha, Jesus, Krishna and the Ultimate Relationship — in the Santa Monica series. 3000 people attended in the 4th or 5th year that I went there. The Santa Monica Civic centre was flooded with people. It is a huge auditorium — accommodating all those 3000 people. So you see, all those who had asked me, "Why do you come here? It is so saturated," were now going, "Oh, wow!"

You see what I am saying? When you have a *sankalpa,* you should stick with it. You should have absolute confidence in your own product.

Guruji, why is it that in front of some people we feel inferior and in front of some others, we feel we are superior to them?
That is because you do not recognise some people. Those who you feel are inferior to you, they may have some secrets which you do not know. You should learn to honour them. Say, your servant maid, who works everyday in your home, you do not know what hidden qualities she may have. And similarly, with people who you think are superior to you, perhaps you do not know them well enough. If there is something good in them, respect them. How you can overcome the complexity is simply by respecting both sets of people. You respect your seniors and juniors alike. Why don't you try this approach?

What is the best quality of a good manager?
I think I have already answered that question. Were you napping at the time? Now that is a good quality in a manager — being able to catch those who are napping! You do not have to bother about those who are working. A manager needs to go around and catch hold of those who are napping.

Some days when I walk around the Ashram, at the international campus, I go up to someone and pinpoint exactly where the problem is and point out what needs correction. I visited our Ayurveda factory after a gap of 2 years. (I rarely visit it!) There I found people explaining what was going on in each room. I pointed to one room and asked, "What is that room for?" They said, "This is a store room where we store all the medicines that have passed their expiry date." I said, "Open that room, I want to see what's in there." When

I went in, I found three big boxes full of medicines which had not expired yet, which had another eight months to go. The expiry date was 2008, August, and it was still January. So I said, "Come on, take these out of the boxes. We can distribute it to people in the villages, we can do something about it."

So my point is, you do not have to bother about those who are really managing things well. As a good manager, you need to direct your attention to where you may find people napping. And sometimes, those of you who have time on your hands, or even after you take up a job when you have some spare time, you should sign up for the Teachers' Training Course — Part 1 and Part 2. It will be a miracle for you to see how your hidden abilities are churned out during these courses. You will love it. There, I give certain exercises to people. For example, I tell them, "In half an hour, you have to plan and execute the menu for a meal for 200 people." We learn how to do team work. There is no time to discuss ideas at length. Usually, if a project is thrown at you, the discussion takes up most of the time. Someone will say, "I will make chapattis," while another will say, "I will cook the rice" and another will say, "I will make this sabji." And in this discussion, precious time is lost. So here, you will not be given that luxury. You will be given just half an hour and then 200 people are going to come right up to your door. They are going to sit there at the dining table and you have to serve them. In that limited time, you have to decide on a menu, you have to prepare the food, you have to serve them, and you have to make sure they all eat. And this is just one of the tasks we give out. There are many such activities and tasks that do not allow you to be dull, they force your entire personality to come alive! You just have to be alive both in your head and in your heart. Those who are alive in the head alone, are dead in the heart. Those who are alive entirely in their heart, emotionally they are quite weak, and they are dead when it comes to using their head.

Guruji, how can practising the Art of Living help us become better managers?

What do you need to manage? Do you need to manage machines or people? People, right? To manage people, you need to be in a pleasant state of mind yourself. For some reason you are not aware of, sometimes you do not feel like talking to certain people. And at other times, for no visible reason, you feel that you want to talk to certain people. Do you know why? Because everyone emits some vibrations — bio-rhythms, these are called. When the bio-rhythms emitted are positive, you feel like talking to them, you feel like working with these people. But if the bio-rhythms emitted are stressed and negative, you take one look at the person and you want to run the other way. What type of a person do you want to be? Do you want to be someone who everyone wants to come and work with, or who everyone wants to run away from? Then you need the Art of Living. Do you see what I am saying?

To manage people, you have got to manage your mind first. You have to keep your spirits high at all times. With low energy levels comes depression and apathy. And that is where YES+ Art of Living programmes help, in changing your energy levels. If you ever come across anyone who seems to have lost interest in life itself, bring them to the Art of Living programme.

We all need to experience a shift in our energy, enthusiasm and attitude. We need to realise that it is possible to achieve this change, and that is what Art of Living does for you.

The Art of Living
&
The International Association for Human Values

Transforming Lives

The Founder

His Holiness Sri Sri Ravi Shankar

His Holiness Sri Sri Ravi Shankar is a universally revered spiritual and humanitarian leader. His vision of a violence-free, stress-free society through the reawakening of human values has inspired millions to broaden their spheres of responsibility and work towards the betterment of the world. Born in 1956 in southern India, Sri Sri was often found deep in meditation as a child. At the age of four, he astonished his teachers by reciting the Bhagavad Gita, an ancient Sanskrit scripture. He has always had the unique gift of presenting the deepest truths in the simplest of words.

Sri Sri established the Art of Living, an educational and humanitarian Non-Governmental Organisation that works in special consultative status with the Economic and Social Council (ECOSOC) of the United Nations in 1981. Present in over 151 countries, it formulates and implements lasting solutions to conflicts and issues faced by individuals, communities and nations. In 1997, he founded the International Association for Human Values (IAHV) to foster human values and lead sustainable development projects. Sri Sri has reached out to more than 300 million people worldwide through personal interactions, public events, teachings, Art of Living workshops and humanitarian initiatives. He has brought to the masses ancient practices which were traditionally kept exclusive, and has designed many self development techniques which can easily be integrated into daily life to calm the mind and instill confidence and enthusiasm. One of Sri Sri's most unique offerings to the world is the Sudarshan Kriya, a powerful breathing technique that facilitates physical, mental, emotional and social well-being.

Numerous honours have been bestowed upon Sri Sri,

including the Order of the Pole Star (the highest state honour in Mongolia), the Peter the Great Award (Russian Federation), the Sant Shri Dnyaneshwara World Peace Prize (India) and the Global Humanitarian Award (USA). Sri Sri has addressed several international forums, including the United Nations Millennium World Peace Summit (2000), the World Economic Forum (2001, 2003) and several parliaments across the globe.

The Art of Living

In Service Around The World

(www.artofliving.org)

The largest volunteer-based network in the world, with a wide range of social, cultural and spiritual activities, the Art of Living has reached out to over 300 million people from all walks of life, since 1982. A non-profit, educational, humanitarian organisation, it is committed to creating peace from the level of the individual upwards, and fostering human values within the global community. Currently, the Art of Living service projects and educational programmes are carried out in over 151 countries. The organisation works in special consultative status with the Economic and Social Council (ECOSOC) of the United Nations, participating in a variety of committees and activities related to health and conflict resolution.

The Art of Living

Stress Elimination Programmes

Holistic Development of Body, Mind & Spirit The Art of Living programmes are a combination of the best of ancient wisdom and modern science. They cater to every age group – children, youth, adults, and every section of society – rural communities, governments, corporate houses, etc. Emphasising holistic living and personal self-development, the programmes facilitate the complete blossoming of an individual's full potential. The cornerstone of all our workshops is the Sudarshan Kriya, a unique, potent breathing practice.

- The Art of Living Course Part I

- The Art of Living Course Part II

- Sahaj Samadhi Meditation

- Divya Samaaj ka Nirmaan (DSN)

- The All Round Training in Excellence
  (ART Excel)

- The Youth Empowerment Seminar (YES!)
  (for 15-18 year old)

- The Youth Empowerment Seminar Plus (YES!+)
  (for 18+ year old)

- The Prison Programme

- Achieving Personal Excellence Program (APEX)
  www.apexprogram.org

- Sri Sri Yoga
  www.srisriyoga.in

International Centres

INDIA

21ˢᵗ KM, Kanakapura Road, Udayapura,
Bangalore – 560 082.
Karnataka.
Telephone : ++91-80-67262626/27/28/29
Email : info@vvmvp.org

CANADA

13 Infinity Road
St. Mathieu du Parc
Quebec G0x 1n0
Telephone : +819- 532-3328
Fax : +819-532-2033
Email : artdevivre@artofliving.org

GERMANY

Bad Antogast 1
D - 77728 Oppenau.
Telephone : +49 7804-910 923
Fax : +49 7804-910 924
Email : artofliving.germany@t-online.de

www.srisriravishankar.org

www.artofliving.org

www.iahv.org

www.5h.org

Other titles published by Arktos:

Beyond Human Rights
by Alain de Benoist

Carl Schmitt Today
by Alain de Benoist

Manifesto for a European Renaissance
by Alain de Benoist & Charles Champetier

The Problem of Democracy
by Alain de Benoist

Germany's Third Empire
by Arthur Moeller van den Bruck

The Arctic Home in the Vedas
by Bal Gangadhar Tilak

Revolution from Above
by Kerry Bolton

The Fourth Political Theory
by Alexander Dugin

Hare Krishna in the Modern World
by Graham Dwyer & Richard J. Cole

Fascism Viewed from the Right
by Julius Evola

Metaphysics of War
by Julius Evola

Notes on the Third Reich
by Julius Evola

The Path of Cinnabar
by Julius Evola

Archeofuturism
by Guillaume Faye

Convergence of Catastrophes
by Guillaume Faye

Why We Fight
by Guillaume Faye

The WASP Question
by Andrew Fraser

We are Generation Identity
by Generation Identity

War and Democracy
by Paul Gottfried

The Saga of the Aryan Race
by Porus Homi Havewala

Homo Maximus
by Lars Holger Holm

The Owls of Afrasiab
by Lars Holger Holm

De Naturae Natura
by Alexander Jacob

Fighting for the Essence
by Pierre Krebs

Can Life Prevail?
by Pentti Linkola

Guillaume Faye and the Battle of Europe
by Michael O'Meara

New Culture, New Right
by Michael O'Meara

The National Rifle Aassociation and the Media
by Brian Anse Patrick

The Ten Commandments of Propaganda
by Brian Anse Patrick

Morning Crafts
by Tito Perdue

A Handbook of Traditional Living
by Raido

The Agni and the Ecstasy
by Steven J. Rosen

The Jedi in the Lotus
by Steven J. Rosen

It Cannot Be Stormed
by Ernst von Salomon

The Outlaws
by Ernst von Salomon

The Dharma Manifesto
by Sri Dharma Pravartaka Acharya

Management Mantras
by Sri Sri Ravi Shankar

Tradition & Revolution
by Troy Southgate

Against Democracy and Equality
by Tomislav Sunic

Nietzsche's Coming God
by Abir Taha

Generation Identity
by Markus Willinger

The Initiate: Journal of Traditional Studies
by David J. Wingfield (ed.)

CPSIA information can be obtained at www.ICGtesting.com
Printed in the USA
BVOW03s1411190614

356843BV00001B/2/P